WHAT ARE THEY SAYING ABOUT
THE UNIVERSAL SALVIFIC WILL OF GOD?

What Are They Saying About the Universal Salvific Will of God?

Josephine Lombardi

PAULIST PRESS
New York/Mahwah, NJ

Much of the material of this book has been reworked from the author's doctoral dissertation, "The Universal Salvific Will of God in Official Documents of the Roman Catholic Church," published in 2007 by The Edwin Mellen Press. The material has been used with the kind permission of The Edwin Mellen Press, Lewiston, New York.

Cover design by James Brisson
Book design by Theresa M. Sparacio

Library of Congress Cataloging-in-Publication Data

Lombardi, Josephine.
    What are they saying about the universal salvific will of God? /Josephine Lombardi.
      p. cm.
    Includes bibliographical references and index.
    ISBN-13: 978-0-8091-4562-1 (alk. paper)
    1. Salvation outside the Catholic Church—History of doctrines. 2. Salvation—Christianity—History of doctrines—20th century. 3. Catholic Church—Doctrines. 4. Catholic Church—Relations. I. Title.
    BT755.L594 2007
    234—dc22

                                     2008012161

Published by Paulist Press
997 Macarthur Boulevard
Mahwah, New Jersey 07430

www.paulistpress.com

Printed and bound in the
United States of America

Contents

Vatican II Document Abbreviations

AG—*Ad Gentes*, Decree on the Mission Activity of the Church, 1965.

DeV—*Dominum et Vivificantem*, Encyclical of Pope John Paul II, On the Holy Spirit in the Life of the Church and the World, 1986.

DH—*Dignitatis Humanae*, Declaration on Religious Freedom, 1965.

DI—*Dominus Iesus*, Declaration on the Unicity and Salvific Universality of Jesus Christ and the Church, 2001.

DP—*Dialogue and Proclamation*, Reflection and Orientations on Inter-religious Dialogue and the Proclamation of the Gospel of Jesus Christ, Pontifical Council for Inter-Religious Dialogue, 1991.

DV—*Dei Verbum*, Dogmatic Constitution on Divine Revelation, 1965.

EN—*Evangelii Nuntiandi*, Apostolic Exhortation of Pope Paul VI, 1975.

GS—*Gaudium et Spes*, Pastoral Constitution on the Church in the Modern World, 1965.

LG—*Lumen Gentium*, Dogmatic Constitution on the Church, 1964.

NA—*Nostra Aetate*, Declaration on the Relation of the Church to Non-Christian Religions, 1965.

ND—J. Neuner and J. Dupuis, eds., *The Christian Faith in the Doctrinal Documents of the Catholic Church*, 7th rev. ed. (New York: Alba House, 2001).

RH—*Redemptor Hominis*, Encyclical of Pope John Paul II, The Redeemer of Man, 1979.

RM—*Redemptoris Missio*, Encyclical of Pope John Paul II, On the Permanent Validity of the Church's Missionary Mandate, 1990.

ST—*Summa Theologiae* of Thomas Aquinas (London: Blackfriars Edition, 1964–76)

UR—*Unitatis Redintegratio*, Decree on Ecumenism, 1964.

Introduction

Since the Council of Trent (1545–63), the official teachings of the Catholic Church have moved away from an exclusive understanding of the universal salvific will of God to one that is increasingly inclusive. This inclusive view affirms that the salvific work of God is present and operative in other religions while maintaining the teaching that Jesus remains the only Savior of all people.

Today Christians are much more aware of the many religions that exist around the world. Roughly two-thirds of the world's population consists of members of non-Christian religious traditions. This reality has encouraged interreligious dialogue among the religions of the world and has challenged the magisterium to communicate better its views on mission and evangelization. Moreover, it has moved the pope, official Vatican congregations, and theologians to reconsider official Church teaching on salvation outside the Church and the universal salvific will of God.

Of special concern for the magisterium has been the challenge of reconciling two essential beliefs in light of the religious diversity that exists, namely, the universal salvific will of God suggested in passages such as 1 Timothy 2:3–4, "This is right and is acceptable in the sight of God our Savior, who desires everyone to be saved and to come to the knowledge of the truth"; and the uniqueness and particularity of Jesus Christ affirmed in texts such

1

as Acts 4:12, "There is salvation in no one else, for there is no other name under heaven given among mortals by which we must be saved." Taken together both claims suggest that Jesus is the only Savior, but that the salvific will of God extends beyond the limits of Christianity. The attempt to uphold both beliefs challenges one to reconcile the claim that God desires all human beings to respond to God's offer of salvation with the claim that salvation is offered only through the work of the person of Jesus Christ. Of the two claims the latter is the more controversial, since much of the human race does not profess belief in Jesus Christ. While some Christian traditions do teach that it is not necessary for one to profess faith in Jesus Christ in order to be saved, others continue to underline the need for explicit belief in Christ.

To teach the universal salvific will of God is to affirm God's desire to offer salvation to all people, even beyond the limits of Christianity. On the one hand, Christians may not hesitate to affirm God's desire to save all people; on the other hand, the teaching that Jesus is the Savior for Christians, Muslims, and Buddhists creates some tension both inside and outside the Church. While God's offer of salvation is universal, the gift of salvation has been accomplished in the person of Jesus Christ. The Triune God has offered the gift of salvation to all people since the beginning of time (NA 4; Ps 67; 68:20; Jer 3:23); however, the magisterium maintains that Jesus is the means of salvation. In other words, he brings about salvation. This in some way suggests that Christianity is unique, as it has been set apart to communicate something special to the world: the accomplishment of salvation in Jesus Christ the Son of God.

God's desire to communicate God's love and will for our fulfillment is universal; however, the belief that Jesus Christ is the only Savior is not as easy to communicate. Teachings on the salvific activity of Jesus Christ have been featured throughout the history of the Church. Of interest here is the other claim that is just as important, namely, that God wills to offer the gift of salvation to all people. This claim, then, has inspired many questions.

What does it mean to preach to all people that God wills their fulfillment, their redemption, and ultimately their salvation? For Christians it is difficult to study and contemplate the universal salvific will of God without referring to the teaching that claims Jesus as Savior. With the growth of dialogue among the religions of the world and an awareness of how these traditions mediate God's grace to their members, Christians with an informed faith life will be challenged to integrate this knowledge with their beliefs about Christ. While in some circles it has been established that God summons all to salvation, regardless of belief, it has not been clarified as to how and whether other religions mediate salvation to their own members. How is God at work in the religions of the world? How does the magisterium defend its claim that Jesus is the only Savior of all creation? And how has the universal salvific will of God been presented in the official teachings of the Catholic Church and in the work of contemporary theologians?

The Significance of This Study

An examination of official Church documents demonstrates the magisterium's attempt to reconcile God's will to save all people with the reality of the billions of non-Christians who populate the earth. The Congregation for the Doctrine of the Faith has encouraged this study, as "theology has importance for the Church in every age so that it can respond to the plan of God 'who desires all men to be saved and to come to the knowledge of the truth' (1 Tim. 2:4)."[1] Consequently, there has been a development in official Church teaching on the universal salvific will of God. While some mention had been made over the centuries of the will of God or God's desire to save all people, for many centuries salvation was tied ultimately to membership in the Church, a valid baptism, and explicit faith in Jesus Christ as Savior. New teachings were developed as awareness of the New World grew and attempts to evangelize people in new lands were met with struggle and sometimes failure.

The teachings of the magisterium manifest a struggle to understand the mercy and love of a God who calls all people to union with God. Conversely, they sometimes manifested an exclusive spirit that limited God's will to save to those who satisfied certain conditions, namely, a valid baptism, an act of faith, and membership in the "true" Church. Hence, what was presented was not the unlimited salvific will of God, but the limited salvific will of the Church. In response, then, to the greater awareness of the New World and the vast numbers of non-Christians, the Church began to develop new teachings. The question of salvation of members of other religions of the world and how one understands their salvific value will depend on how one understands the universal salvific will of God. Some Christian traditions have limited the universal salvific will of God while others see God's desire to save all people as limitless. Theologians, as well, have put forward different paradigms that address this question. Their insights are helpful in situating the official documents of the Catholic Church. Theologians such as J. P. Schineller,[2] Paul F. Knitter,[3] Allan Race, and Jacques Dupuis[4] speak of three paradigms, namely, exclusivism, inclusivism, and pluralism, paralleled by ecclesiocentrism, Christocentrism, and theocentrism.

Christians who find themselves in the exclusivist camp claim that people must, in faith, explicitly accept the teaching that Jesus is the only Savior, and through the grace of God through Christ they can hope to be saved (Rom 1:20; 2:15; 2:23; Mark 1:14–15; 16:15–16; 3:29; 2 Thess 1:9; 1 Cor 1:18). The claim that upholds the universality and particularity of Christ arises "formally from the place assigned to Jesus in the New Testament."[5] The New Testament refers to Jesus as Savior and makes the connection between him and salvation. In the Catholic Church exclusivism has ecclesiocentric roots as well. As will be discussed in the following chapter, for centuries the Catholic Church upheld the axiom *extra ecclesiam nulla salus* (outside the Church no salvation). In these cases the Church emphasized the need for a valid baptism, faith, and Church membership. The Church mediated salvation and would determine who could be saved. This exclusivist and ecclesiocentric understanding of the universal salvific will of God prevailed for many centuries.

While contemporary Catholic teaching is not exclusivistic, that is, it allows for salvation outside Christianity and outside the limits of the visible Church, it continues to claim a mediatory role for the Church. As will be discussed in chapter 3, the Second Vatican Council refers to the Church as the "universal sacrament of salvation"[6] and speaks of the necessity of Church for salvation.[7] Nevertheless, official and contemporary Church teaching is inclusive. However, some official documents are ambiguous.

Inclusivism affirms the universal salvific will of God and recognizes that God's offer of saving grace is extended to members of other religious traditions (1 Tim 2:4; 4:10; 1:15; John 3:16–17; 1:9; 12:32; Luke 15; 2 Pet 3:9). However, in official documents of the Catholic Church, this paradigm is closely linked to the claim that Jesus is the only Savior. Contemporary official teaching upholds a trinitarian inclusivism whereby salvation is extended to all people through God's initiative, the salvific activity of Jesus and the Holy Spirit. People who follow other faiths may be saved through following God's will and the dictates of their conscience;[8] however, their salvation is due to the work of Jesus Christ and the activity of the Holy Spirit. Inspired by early Christian writers, official documents speak of the work of the *Logos* before the Christ-event. Inclusivists declare that the *Logos*, or the Word, existed and was actively inspiring people prior to the incarnation (John 1:9). Through the work of the *Logos* God was at work redemptively in the lives of all people from the time of creation. In some ways, then, *Logos* Christology is the foundation of inclusivism. Official Church teaching sets out to uphold the universal salvific will of God and the roles of Jesus and the Spirit in the salvation of humanity.

Paul F. Knitter offers this commentary on the present Catholic approach to salvation:

> The Catholic approach recognizes both revelation and salvation outside Christ and Christianity; it admits that Christ need not be considered the constitutive cause, the sole vehicle of God's saving love in the world. It continues to affirm, however, that Christ must be proclaimed as the fullest revelation, the definitive savior; the norm above all other norms for religions. This, they say, is as far as Christians can go. To go beyond this point is to jeopardize the distinctiveness, the essence, of Christianity.[9]

Hence in this position the two truth claims must be upheld: God desires to save all people through the mediation of Jesus Christ.

In the pluralist paradigm, however, multiple saviors are affirmed and religions are considered ways of salvation as they can mediate salvation to their own members without the work of an external figure. While there are a variety of spectrums within each of these views, the soteriocentric pluralistic view, as upheld by Knitter,[10] supports interreligious dialogue, the reign of God, salvation, human fulfillment, and social and ecological justice. God has one plan for all people although it is communicated in unique ways by different mediators and religious traditions. In the pluralistic paradigm,

> all religions and world views are historically conditioned, relative to various stages of historical development and as such cannot claim ultimate allegiance, nor promise an ultimate truth nor an ultimate salvation. In a pluralistic perspective, no particular religion can ever be the unique and only religion of mankind.[11]

Pluralism has challenged both exclusivists and inclusivists to reconsider God's salvific action throughout the religions of the world. Christians are called to inform their theological reflection with dialogue and mutual reflection. Pluralism, then, moves people to address the value of other religions in light of the universal salvific will of God:

> Other religions may be just as effective and successful in bringing their followers to truth, peace, and well being with God as Christianity has been for Christians;...these other religions, again because they are so different from Christianity, may have just as important a message and vision for all peoples as Christianity does...Only if Christians are truly open to the possibility that there are many true, saving religions and that Christianity is one among many ways in which God has touched and transformed our world, only then can authentic dialogue take place.[12]

The pluralist paradigm, then, challenges the Church to make a distinction between evangelization and authentic dialogue. Thus the Church is challenged to reconsider its views on salvation and members of other religions.

Clarifying the Universal Salvific Will of God

The universal salvific will of God is the part of Christian doctrine that focuses on the infinite nature of divine goodness and holiness. It is the idea that God offers salvation to all people, but that all people need to respond to it in faith. Salvation is offered through the "gratuitous grace of God,"[13] whose desire to save is universal. This teaching has its biblical foundation in 1 Timothy 2:3–4: "This is right and is acceptable in the sight of God our Savior, who desires everyone to be saved and to come to the knowledge of the truth." Other texts that support this teaching are Matthew 26:28; Mark 10:45; and Romans 11:32. While this doctrine has not been solemnly defined, the magisterium continues to uphold the universality of God's desire to save all people.

Similarly, the Second Vatican Council declared, "God graciously arranged that the things he had once revealed for the salvation of all peoples should remain in their entirety, throughout the ages, and be transmitted to all generations."[14] The universal salvific will of God is part of every person's destiny, so God extends this possibility to all people. This desire to save all people was "held out" to all people, even when "they had fallen in Adam."[15] Furthermore, God's will is grounded in hope. Karl Rahner writes:

> God has empowered us and laid the obligation on us…of hoping for final salvation for all men, whom we must love, and consequently for ourselves. This means that we are to affirm the saving will of God which is implied and as it is implied in this act of hope. Hope of course is meant in the sense already described, of an absolutely fundamental act of personal life.[16]

Although hope in salvation for all is key in this teaching, Rahner points out that scripture does not support the theory of *apocatastasis,* which presents the idea that all people will be saved.[17] Instead, he notes, scripture presents two possibilities for humankind: salvation or perdition (Matt 25:31–45). Hence, Rahner goes on to affirm that the official teaching of the Church, following scripture, rejects the doctrine of *apocatastasis.* God offers the gift of salvation; however, human beings are free to accept it or reject it.

The universal salvific will of God has been discussed in *Christianity and the World Religions,* a document issued in 1997 by the International Theological Commission. The document declares that the "God who wishes to save all is the Father of our Lord Jesus Christ." Furthermore, God's desire to save all people preceded the creation of the world (cf. Eph 1:3–10). This salvific will is rooted in God's "infinite love and tenderness." God is the Savior who calls all people to the truth. Thus, again we hear how the universal salvific will of God extends back to the creation of the world, and calls all people to "recognize the truth" and to "adhere to the faith."

The commission goes on to declare that the "gifts which God offers all men for directing themselves to salvation…are rooted in his salvific will." Moreover, it affirms that "even non-Christians" are included in the "universal call to salvation."

In another more recent study, *The Hope of Salvation,* completed by the International Theological Commission in 2007, theologians set out to examine God's desire to save all people, even unbaptized infants. While the document focused on the theory of limbo, it provides a good overview of how we are to understand the universal salvific will of God. The commission attempts to reconcile two sets of biblical affirmations: texts affirming the universal salvific will of God (1 Tim 2:4) and those regarding the necessity of baptism (Mark 16:16; Matt 28:18–19). Throughout the text, the commission affirms the universality of God's desire to save us:

> The universality of the saving will of God the Father as realized through the unique and universal mediation of his Son, Jesus Christ, is forcefully expressed in the first letter of Timothy…The emphatic reiteration of "all" (vv. 1, 4, 6), and the justification of this universality on the basis of the uniqueness of God and of his mediator who himself is a man, suggests that nobody is excluded from this salvific will. Insofar as it is the object of prayer (cf. 1 Tim 2:1), this salvific will refers to a will which is sincere on the part of God, but, at times is resisted by human beings. (46)

The conclusion of this study "gives rise to the hope that there is a path to salvation for infants who die without baptism"; therefore, these infants may be saved and "brought to eternal happiness." While the theory of limbo is not included in the *Catechism of the Catholic Church* (1992), the commission prepared this study in response to a growing pastoral need for clarification on the fate of unbaptized infants. The *Catechism* teaches that infants who die without baptism "are entrusted by the church to the mercy of God." Nevertheless, the commission set out to clarify this teaching, noting that there are "serious theological and liturgical grounds for hope that unbaptized infants who die will be saved." Hence, the universal salvific will of God extends to people of all ages regardless of baptism. It is in this way, writes William G. Most, that the salvific will of God is universal and sincere:

> But we, along with all Catholic theologians today, know that the universal salvific will is sincere. We know this because of the clarity of many passages of Scripture quoted above, and because of the teachings of the Fathers of the Church. But we can also show in another way that the will is beyond doubt sincere, namely, with the help of other passages of Scripture…to will salvation to anyone for his own sake is to love him. In other words, the salvific will is really one aspect, and the chief expression, of the love of God for men. Therefore, if we ask whether the salvific will is sincere, it is the same as asking whether the love of God for men is sincere. But it would be one of the worst heresies to deny that God sincerely loves all men. Therefore, the salvific will is sincere, and is not a mere signified will, nor a mere metaphor.[18]

God's will to save all people is sincere and it extends to members of all religions. This book will examine how the universal salvific will of God has been understood in relation to members of other religious traditions.

Overview

In examining key documents and the work of contemporary theologians, this book traces a step-by-step development that marks the movement away from exclusivistic views toward an inclusive understanding of the universal salvific will of God. Step one includes the view expressed in the axiom *extra ecclesiam nulla salus*. This view was widely held until the discovery of the New World and the Council of Trent. Step two consists of the teaching presented at the Council of Trent that affirmed salvation for members of other religions through baptism of desire. This council taught that a desire for baptism, whether explicit or implicit, would suffice for salvation. Step three took place at the end of the nineteenth century and into the twentieth century when Pius IX and Pius XII developed the teaching on inculpable ignorance. These two teachings, namely, salvation through baptism of desire and inculpable ignorance, asserted the mercy of God, who will not condemn those who live and worship inculpably outside the Church. Moreover, several popes, in their struggle against Jansenism, taught that God's salvific grace is available to those outside the Church. However, it was not until the Second Vatican Council (1962–65) that the bishops of the Church took a huge step, collectively affirming the universal salvific will of God and the work of God's grace in other religions.

This fourth step in the development of Church teaching is that God honors those who seek the divine will, following their consciences as they hold to what is "true" and "holy" in their own religious traditions. The Second Vatican Council, then, went on to speak positively about other religions and affirmed the teaching that God wills to save all people and offers God's grace to all in the hope that people will respond to this offer of salvation. Moreover, the council offered a preview into what would become a theology of the Holy Spirit when the official documents of the Church go on to explain how the action of the Spirit brings salvation to the religions of the world.

The third chapter explores ways in which documents issued during the pontificate of John Paul II addressed whether other religions are a means of salvation. Step five marks the Church's attempt to understand whether other religions represent "ways" of salvation. Here I examine the teaching of John Paul II and his discussion of the work of the Holy Spirit in the religions of the world. It is in his work that the discussion of the Holy Spirit begins to develop. It is the action of the Holy Spirit that facilitates salvation for members of other religions. I also consider other more recent views put forward by other official Vatican congregations during his pontificate and the first years of Benedict XVI's pontificate. It is in this chapter that we begin to see how the magisterium is challenged to affirm whether other religions are mediators of salvation.

The remaining chapters consider views put forward by contemporary Catholic and Protestant theologians. How the idea of the universal salvific will of God relates to the religions of the world is a topic that has caused quite a stir among theologians. While many scholars have addressed this topic, in such a short study it would be impossible to exhaust the contributions made by all of them. Among Catholic scholars I have chosen to present the views of Jacques Dupuis, Paul F. Knitter, and Gavin D'Costa. These authors represent a range of views and have made important contributions to the recent discussion on the universal salvific will of God and other religions. Among Protestant scholars I include the views of Clark Pinnock, S. Mark Heim, and John Hick. The goal is to provide a discussion of contemporary thinkers who have served to shape the current debate surrounding this topic.

Official documents of the Church have an enormous influence over Christians. Those considered here represent the ongoing effort to articulate the truth about the universal salvific will of God and God's saving work among the religions of the world. The question of how God provides for all people to be saved has been met with mixed response. Here the work of theologians is necessary.

1
Historical Steps toward Inclusivity

The current discussion on the universal salvific will of God
cannot be appreciated unless it is studied in the light of historical
developments. In this chapter I include a historical survey of
papal and conciliar decrees and canons of the past, leading up to
the Second Vatican Council (1962–65), which address this topic.
From the early Church to the twentieth century, official Church
teaching centered mostly on the role of the Church as mediator of
salvation. Salvation was tied to orthodox belief and orthodox
teachings that could only be found in the true Church. God's
desire to save all people depended heavily on Church membership, belief in the teachings of the orthodox faith, and the grace
received during baptism. Hence, God's will to save all people was
limited due to these conditions.

God willed the salvation of all people, but the Church would
determine how and where. However, from time to time it would
be the mercy of God that would inspire thinkers to develop new
teachings. To be sure, the development of teaching on this topic
spans centuries; hence, it is important to see how the Church
came to teach on the issue of the universal salvific will of God.
This chapter maps out the first three steps in the Church's development on the teaching of the universal salvific will of God and
salvation outside the Church. Thus, we will see how the official
documents of the Church moved from proclaiming *extra eccle-*

siam nulla salus, to salvation through baptism of desire, and, finally, to salvation in Christ through inculpable ignorance.

Step One: *Extra Ecclesiam Nulla Salus*

The early church fathers did not limit their concern for the salvation of souls to those who lived after the Christ-event. Instead, some early Christian writers developed theologies that allowed for the possibility of salvation for both Jews and Gentiles who had died before the time of Christ. These theologies came in response to questions that were posed to early Christians. Jews and Gentiles asked early Christians why the Savior of the world came only recently into the world. They were concerned about the fate of souls who lived and died before this Savior. It has been contended that it is the prologue of the Gospel according to John (1:1–5) that lays the foundation for the responses given to the above questions.

The awareness of the presence of God through God's Word has influenced some early writers' teachings on the universal salvific will of God. The use and presentation of the *Logos,* or Word, as Christ had immense influence on theological thinking on God's will to save all people from the beginning of time. *Logos*-theology has continued to influence the study of the history of salvation. Several early writers used it in their attempts to understand the mystery of the salvific will of God.

In the second and third centuries of the Common Era, writers such as Justin Martyr, Irenaeus, and Clement of Alexandria developed various *Logos*-theologies based on the prologue of the Gospel according to John. These writers addressed the issue of the universal salvific will of God and provided insights that would later contribute to the Church's teaching on the topic. The first centuries in the history of Christianity saw the development of the doctrine on the person of Jesus Christ, his place in the Trinity, and the accomplishment of God's plan to save all people through him.

The First Council of Constantinople (381 CE) established the consubstantiality and coeternity of the three divine persons. This same council declared that Jesus Christ was "before the ages fully God the Word, and that in the last days he became fully man for the sake of our salvation." For the "sake of our salvation" the Word became man in the person of Jesus Christ. The Word, as early writers contended, allowed for faithful Jews and Gentiles to be saved before the Christ event. However, those who died after the Christ-event had other conditions to satisfy. For example, the First Council of Constantinople stressed the importance of embracing orthodoxy and baptism. However, even before this council, writers such as Ignatius of Antioch (d. 110 CE), Ambrose of Milan (d. 397 CE), and Origen (185–253 CE) put forward reasons why those who had not embraced orthodoxy or the true Church would be denied entrance into the kingdom of God. Such views were based on literal interpretations of various scriptural texts that limit salvation to those who hold explicit faith in Christ and are saved by the waters of baptism. The New Testament is, at times, quite clear regarding the need for baptism for salvation (for example, John 3:5; Mark 16:15–16; Acts 2:37-41). Moreover, other texts affirm that salvation is in Christ alone (Acts 4:12). Membership in the orthodox faith then required a proper baptism. Another key text that influenced early writers and papal teaching is 1 Peter 3:18–22, where Peter draws a comparison between those who were saved by the ark of Noah and Christians who are saved through the waters of baptism. Early Christian writers came to use this comparison as a foundation for their teaching that "outside the ark there is no salvation."

Such interpretations led to the development of an axiom that would describe the fate of the many people who find themselves outside the Church. While the axiom *extra ecclesiam nulla salus* had been used by other writers, it is Cyprian of Carthage who is responsible for the interpretation of the axiom. Cyprian, like other thinkers, directed the axiom to those who left the Church willingly. Heretics were guilty for separating themselves from the Church. However, the first four centuries saw Christianity become the official religion of the Roman Empire and with the spread of Christianity came the expectation that more people would join the Church.

The expansion of the kingdom was supposed to encourage more and more people to become baptized Christians. Since it was believed that the gospel had been proclaimed, those who refused to enter the Church were guilty; hence, unwilling Jews and pagans shared in the guilt of heretics. Conversely, all those who wished to abandon their former beliefs were welcomed. The Church welcomed heretics and those belonging to other religions to convert to Christianity. The gospel had been presented to them and it was God's desire that they embrace orthodoxy. Unlike the Jews and Gentiles who lived before the Christ-event, those who lived and died after the event and chose not to enter the Church were found to be guilty of the willful rejection of orthodoxy. For surely God could not punish those who were innocent; thus, those who refused to join the Church were responsible for their own damnation. From this time until the twentieth century, much emphasis was placed on Church membership. The Church then becomes the mediator of salvation. While God's will to save all people is universal, the desire to be saved was not, at least not for some of the church fathers. Augustine of Hippo (354–430 CE) and later Fulgentius of Ruspe presented certain claims that would influence official Church teaching for many centuries.

Similar to Cyprian, Augustine insisted that those who refused to enter the Church were guilty of willful separation and rejection of the Church. He suggested that these people chose to be on the outside of the true Church. In effect, Augustine placed limits on God's power. Augustine believed that the salvific grace of God was extended to all people but not all people would accept it. For him, God provides the means through which people can be saved; however, those who refuse to make use of God's offer are outside the possibility for salvation. A person is free to choose or reject God's grace. For Augustine, then, it is the use of our free will that counters God's desire to save all people. Hence, God knows the intentions of one's heart and condemns those who fail to "come to grace." Even before one chooses, God knows whether one will accept or reject God's offer. For Augustine, all people have the choice to accept God's grace and be saved or to reject God's offer and be damned. Augustine seals the exclusivist understanding of the axiom *extra ecclesiam nulla salus* and limits an understanding of the universal salvific will of God. However, a century later, it would be Fulgentius of Ruspe's use of the axiom that would go on to influence official Church teaching.

Fulgentius's interpretation of the axiom *extra ecclesiam nulla salus* further emphasized the exclusion from salvation of all those who were not among the faithful. He wrote that Jews, heretics, and schismatics will "go into the eternal fire 'which was prepared for the devil and his angels' (Mt. 25:41)."[1] Here Fulgentius, using scripture as his source, condemns all people who find themselves outside the Catholic Church to the fires of hell— words that would be used by Eugene IV in the Decree for the Copts prepared for the General Council of Florence in 1442. However, before we discuss this document, let us review how other popes and councils, before this time, addressed the issue of the universal salvific will of God.

A misuse of scripture (Matt 25:41) and the conviction that the Church was necessary for salvation would propel the axiom into the Middle Ages, where it came to be bound up with the papacy. There are a number of medieval texts that make the connection between Church and salvation. The mercy of God and God's desire to save all people was limited, since entrance into heaven was limited to a select few.

We begin our discussion of the Middle Ages with Innocent III's letter (December 18, 1208) to the archbishop of Taragona. The letter urges the Waldensian Durandus de Osca to return to the Roman Church. Upon his return he would be asked to accept this profession of faith: "We heartily believe and orally confess the one church, not of heretics, but the holy, Roman, Catholic, apostolic (church), outside of which, we believe, no one is saved."[2] While Innocent III made use of the axiom in his letter, the Fourth Lateran Council (1215 CE) was the first ecumenical council to use the axiom: "There is indeed one universal church of the faithful, outside of which nobody at all is saved."[3]

Hence, the Church officially teaches that there is no salvation outside the Church. While God desired to save all people, Church leadership continued to place restrictions on how people could be saved. The Church would decide who could be saved and why. The authority of the pope grew and it would be Boniface VIII who, in the bull *Unam Sanctum* (1302), would put forward the idea that salvation was tied to obedience to the pope.

In response to the defiance of Philip IV of France Boniface issued the bull in which he claims authority over kings in secular as well as spiritual matters. In this bull there are two main concerns, namely, the constitution of the Church and the need to belong to it, and the need to understand and accept the powers that flow from the Church: "Furthermore we declare, state and define that it is absolutely necessary for the salvation of all people that they submit to the Roman Pontiff."[4] While the axiom continued to be upheld, another development emerged: submission to the pope is necessary for salvation.

As time went on the doctrine that there is no salvation outside the Catholic Church continued to be taught. The Decree for the Copts (1442) of the General Council of Basel-Ferrara-Florence-Rome (1431–45) represents another attempt to reinforce the axiom *extra ecclesiam nulla salus*. This council was summoned by Eugenius IV as a council of reunion. Directed, then, to Christians in the East and West, the documents of this council contain many references to the necessity of faith in Jesus Christ and the teachings of the Catholic Church: "Whoever wills to be saved, before all things it is necessary that he hold the Catholic faith."[5] However, one of its decrees, a bull prepared by Eugene IV for the reunion of the Copts with the Roman Church, contains a summary of Christian belief in which the traditional axiom is interpreted most rigidly. The words of the decree are familiar, as they are borrowed from Fulgentius of Ruspe's *Treatise on Faith*:

> (The Holy Roman Church)…firmly believes, professes and preaches that all those who are outside the catholic church, not only pagans but also Jews or heretics and schismatics, cannot share in eternal life and will go into the everlasting fire which was prepared for the devil and his angels, unless they are joined to the catholic church before the end of their lives.[6]

It is important to note here that this is the first official document in which besides those who have separated themselves from the Church, Jews and pagans are added to the list of the damned. Separation from the Church means separation from Christ, hence no salvation. It was believed, once again, that all people had received God's offer of grace and that they had been given the opportunity to join the Church; unfortunately, not all would accept. This belief reinforced a negative attitude toward members of other traditions and religions. The negative treatment of those who were sure to have received an opportunity to be saved would be challenged by the discovery of the New World. Here we will see how the medieval worldview had to respond to the discoveries of the fifteenth and sixteenth centuries. It is also here that we see the movement toward the second step in the development of official teaching on the universal salvific will of God and salvation outside the Church. The Church was faced more urgently with the question of how the universal salvific will of God applied to those who had no knowledge of it.

Step Two: Baptism of Desire

The new knowledge that people lived in places where the gospel had not been preached caused Christian writers to reexamine their views toward people "outside the Church." In the span of fifty years the Church went from being sure of its condemnation of all heretics, Jews, and pagans (1442) to being utterly confused when it learned that the world was not coextensive with Christendom (1492).

The discovery of the New World forced theologians to reconsider the requisites for salvation. The necessity of faith and baptism could no longer be held as universal, as so many people had never heard the gospel preached. Theologians needed to find a way to retain the teaching of God's universal salvific will (1 Tim 2:4) and the necessity of faith (Heb 11:6). Thomas Aquinas, writing in the thirteenth century, opened the way for a theory that would account for the salvation of those who had not heard of Jesus Christ. Following Hebrews 11:6 Aquinas writes:

> Whoever would draw near to God must believe that he exists and that he rewards those who seek him. It must be said that in every day and age and for everyone it has always been necessary to believe explicitly in these two things.[7]

Hence, belief and faith in God bring reward even if these two things occur outside the Church. The move toward baptism of desire begins with the acknowledgment of one's desire to seek God and that God "rewards those who seek him."

In the *Summa Theologica* Aquinas develops a theory of baptism of desire, explicit or implicit, that would allow for the salvation of those people who had not received the sacrament of baptism. In one case, Aquinas held that if a person who had accepted the gospel message died before her baptism, she would be saved due to her desire to be baptized.[8] In another case, one that went on to influence official Church teaching, Aquinas considered the situation in which a person who had not heard of Christ desired to follow the will of God. The desire to conform to the will of God would grant him the means by which to be saved. Faith in Christ was implicit in faith in God.[9] Hence, God's grace and offer of forgiveness are made available to the sincere person even before baptism. An implicit or explicit desire for baptism suggests that a person is open to doing God's will. Thus, the universal salvific will of God extends to those who desire to be close to God either through an explicit faith in Christ and the sacrament of baptism or through an implicit faith and the desire to do God's will:

> The sacrament of baptism may be wanting to someone in two ways. First, both in reality and in desire; as is the case with those who neither are baptized, nor wish to be baptized...Second, the sacrament of baptism may be wanting to anyone in reality but not in desire...Such a man can obtain salvation without being actually baptized on account of his desire for baptism. (ST III, q. 68, a. 2, corpus)

Here, Aquinas establishes two ways in which we are to understand baptism of desire.

The challenges of the New World led theologians to develop theories that addressed the issue of universal salvation. Eventually, Aquinas's theory of baptism of desire was adopted by the Council of Trent (1545–63). It is this council that makes it official teaching. This breakthrough, inspired by the discovery of the New World, causes a shift away from exclusive views on the universal salvific will of God and toward views that are more inclusive.

The Council of Trent, called to address the need for reform, opened at Trent, Italy, on December 13, 1545, and closed there on December 4, 1563, having held twenty-five sessions. Paul III called for the council, initiating an agenda for change. Apart from responding to the challenge of the Protestant Reformation, the council set out to address abuses, condemn heresy, defend Catholic doctrine, reform any teachings and practices that smacked of superstition, and restore church identity. However, of concern here is the Decree on Justification (1547).

As was mentioned, this council was called to meet the crisis of the Protestant Reformation and to address the concerns of other reformers who were working within the tradition. It is in this context of confusion and division that the council is to be understood. Not only was the Church faced with the challenge of the discovery of unevangelized peoples, it was now burdened with the tragedy of more schisms, hence loss of membership and loss of saved souls. On baptism, or the desire for it, the council explained:

> After the promulgation of the Gospel, the transition (from the state in which one is born a child of the first Adam to the state of grace and adoption as God's children) cannot take place without the bath of regeneration or the desire for it *(eius voto)*. As it is written: "Unless one is born of water and the Spirit, one cannot enter the kingdom of God" (Jn 3:5).[10]

Here the council affirms the possibility of salvation through baptism of desire. While the council declares that Jesus is the "source of eternal salvation," the above text is not clear as to whether explicit faith in Christ and an explicit desire for baptism are necessary. Instead, the council documents speak of the necessity of faith in God, "who is the rewarder of those who seek him" (Heb 11:6) and the desire for baptism would suffice for justification. Thus, the suggestions of Aquinas that an implicit faith in God and a desire for baptism would be pleasing to God are taken into consideration in this decree. The teaching on baptism of desire, then, affirms the universal salvific will of God and sees a way of salvation for the many people who find themselves outside the Church. By the eighteenth century many Christians became aware of how many inhabitants of the world were members of other faith communities. The fate of their souls was of great interest to the Catholic Church.

The Jansenists posed a challenge to the Catholic Church, as they taught that God's grace was limited to the Church. Two popes addressed this challenge and affirmed God's desire to save people outside the Church. Alexander VIII in 1690 and Clement XI in 1713 taught that God's grace is granted outside the Church.

Clement held that pagans, Jews, and others "do receive the motions of grace by which they can be saved" *(Unigenitus Dei Filius)*. Those who found themselves outside the Church would be given the grace they needed to be saved. However, it is implied that God's grace would lead people to salvation through the Church. The Church needed to reconcile the belief that God willed the salvation of all people (1 Tim 2:4) with the fact that much of the world's population had not converted to Christianity.

Step Three: Inculpable Ignorance

In his allocution *Singulari Quadam* (1854) Pius IX finds a way to bridge the gap between the two claims that God wills the salvation of all people and the necessity of an explicit faith in Jesus Christ through membership in the Church. While affirming the necessity of the Church for salvation, this document is the first to speak of invincible ignorance as a reason for being excused from joining the Church, thus bringing us to the third step in the development of official teaching.

While Pius IX was defending the Church against "the error of indifferentism" and the teaching that the Church was necessary for salvation, he understood that God was just and could not condemn the innocent:

> It must, of course, be held as of faith that no one can be saved outside the Apostolic Roman Church, that the Church is the only ark of salvation, and that whoever does not enter it will perish in the flood. Yet, on the other hand, it must likewise be held as certain that those who are in ignorance of the true religion, if this ignorance is invincible, are not subject to any guilt in this matter before the eyes of the Lord. Now, who could presume for oneself the ability to set the boundaries for such ignorance, taking into consideration the natural differences between peoples, lands, talents and so many other factors? Only when we have been released

> from the bonds of this body and "shall see God as he is" (1 Jn
> 3:2) shall we understand how closely and wonderfully the
> divine mercy and justice are linked. But, as long as we dwell
> on earth, encumbered by the mortal body that dulls our soul,
> let us tenaciously hold the Catholic doctrine that there is
> "one God, one faith, one baptism" (cf. Eph 4:5). To push our
> inquiry further is not right.[11]

This admission that God is merciful toward those who are
invincibly ignorant is a clear departure from the teaching put forward in the Decree for the Copts in 1442. Pius IX is the first to
present the official teaching that *extra ecclesiam nulla salus*
means no salvation for those who culpably find themselves outside the Church. In his encyclical letter *Quanto Conficiamur
Moerere* (1863), he continues to put forward his teaching on the
necessity of the Church for salvation and his teaching on invincible ignorance. Here the pope extends his teaching to non-Catholic
Christians as well as members of other religions:

> We all know that those who suffer from invincible ignorance
> with regard to our holy religion, if they carefully keep the
> precepts of the natural law which have been written by God
> in the hearts of human beings, if they are prepared to obey
> God, and if they lead a virtuous and dutiful life, can, by the
> power of the divine light and grace, attain eternal life.[12]

Once again the mercy of God is featured and it is later noted that
God alone knows "the minds and souls, the thoughts and habits of
all people." Accordingly, God wills to save all people and will not
condemn the innocent.

The issue of membership continues to be developed in the
next century when Pius XII makes a distinction between those
who are members of the Church in reality and those who are
related to the Church in desire and resolution. To this point the
official teaching of the Church has made some advancement in
the question of whether those outside the Church can be saved.

The Council of Trent officially taught the possibility of baptism of desire, and Pius IX officially presents the doctrine of "invincible ignorance." With each of these developments the notion of church is challenged. How one defines and interprets one's understanding of church will determine how one understands the meaning of the axiom. Pius XII's understanding of church is more developed than that found in the writings of other popes and councils we have considered thus far. The encyclical *Mystici Corporis* (1943) further develops the meaning of the axiom *extra ecclesiam nulla salus*.

This encyclical is based on the idea that the Roman Catholic Church, and it alone, is the mystical body of Christ. Hence, only members of the Roman Catholic Church can be members of the church.[13] However, in section 101 of the encyclical, Pius XII suggests the possibility of salvation for those who desire the truth. Further, those who do not belong to the visible structure of the Church are related to it through "desire and longing." While those who find themselves outside the Church cannot be "secure about their salvation" they may still be ordained to the mystical body of Christ through an "unconscious desire and longing." Here the language is ambiguous but it leaves room for the possibility of salvation. Some theologians have suggested that an "unconscious desire" to belong to the Church refers to a person's sincere intention to do God's will.[14] This desire, it seems, applies to both non-Catholic Christians and members of other religions.[15]

Conclusion

We have observed how the awareness of the billions of people who live and die "outside the Church" has challenged Christian thinkers to reconsider their views on the universal salvific will of God and their understanding of what it means to belong to the Church. When one reads that God desires to save all people (1 Tim 2:4), one is called to consider the needs of all of God's creation.

Clearly, Christian writers attempted to reconcile God's universal salvific will with teachings that condemned much of the world's population to the "eternal fires of hell." Official interpretation of the axiom *extra ecclesiam nulla salus* has moved away from a rigid, narrow, and pessimistic view to one that is more open and inclusive, thus coming closer to an understanding of the salvific will of God that is more universal and less limited. While magisterial teaching from the Second Vatican Council to the pontificate of John Paul II is the focus of the following chapter, it has been important to see how the positive developments made at the Second Vatican Council were born out of centuries of theological inquiry. To be sure, theories that emerged, some as early as in the first three centuries, continued to be considered throughout the following centuries. When one studies how the axiom has been interpreted over the centuries, one can detect a development of doctrine. The role of the Church in the salvation of people is still important; however, how one establishes what constitutes Church membership has been expressed differently.

It may seem confusing when, on the one hand, Catholics are taught the necessity of belonging to the Church, and, on the other, they are taught that millions outside the Church can be saved due to the limitless mercy of God. One is expected to reconcile the teaching that the Church mediates salvation with the teaching on the universal salvific will of God that sees no limits.

In the following chapter I note how the council declared that the Church is "necessary for salvation" (LG 14); it is the "general instrument of salvation" (UR 3); and it is the "instrument of salvation of all" (LG 9). Thus, the Church is defined as the "universal sacrament of salvation" (LG 48), that is, "of communion with God and unity among all beings" (LG 1). Still, however, questions remain as to how to understand the "necessity" of the Church as mediator in light of texts such as 1 Timothy 2:5, which attribute the "one mediation" to Jesus Christ himself. How does one reconcile the teaching that God saves all people through his Son Jesus Christ (John 3:16–17) with the teaching that the Church is "necessary for salvation"? Perhaps the council set out to show how all people are, somehow, related to the Church and thus this implies that the Church continues to play a role in mediating salvation to all people. Other Christians are joined to us through baptism and members of other religious traditions are related to the mystical body of Christ through doing God's will.

God desires to save all people. For Christians this universal desire is transmitted through the work of Jesus Christ and the Spirit. The following chapter looks at how the Second Vatican Council and magisterial teaching during the pontificate of John Paul II understood the universal salvific will of God. Let us examine, then, the fourth and fifth steps in the development of official teaching.

2
Magisterial Teaching: The Second Vatican Council to the Pontificate of Benedict XVI

In the previous chapter I examined the development of official Church teaching on the universal salvific will of God from the early Church to the twentieth century. A shift was detected as official documents moved away from an exclusivist understanding to an increasingly inclusive understanding of salvation outside the Church. This inclusive view was due in part to the discovery of the New World and to the increasing awareness of the vast number of people who may never profess an explicit faith in Jesus Christ. In the twentieth century, Pius XII offered an official response to the question of salvation outside the Church that emphasized teachings on baptism of desire and inculpable ignorance.

Step Four: The Presence of God's Grace in Other Religious Traditions

An even larger step forward in the discussion on the universal salvific will of God was taken at the Second Vatican Council (1962–65). Here, in this fourth step, the council confirmed Christian teaching on God's universal offer of grace and salvation (1 Tim 2:4) and it applied this teaching to the various religions outside Christianity. Hence, the council approaches the religions of the world with more openness.

In keeping with the Church's conciliar tradition, the Second Vatican Council opened in response to the concerns of the modern world and to John XXIII's own concern with the inner life of the Church. John XXIII (1958–63) called this ecumenical council three months after his election. This council was a seven-year event from 1959 to 1965. The pope consulted 2,500 bishops, 156 superiors general of religious communities, and 62 theological faculties. John XXIII was convinced that the time had come for a renewing and updating—an *aggiornamento* of the Church. Hence, his two main objectives were internal reform and improved dialogue with other Christian churches.

The Second Vatican Council, from the beginning, was defined by John XXIII as a pastoral, not a doctrinal, council. This means that the council did not set out to define a doctrine. Conversely, past councils had set out to condemn errors and define dogmas. Nevertheless, the conciliar texts of this council are important as they have more authority than ordinary declarations of the papal magisterium, such as encyclicals. It is for this reason that the documents issued by the council must be considered as lending an authoritative voice in the discussion on the universal salvific will of God.

In 1963, Paul VI took over and continued the work of the council. Sixteen documents were produced that addressed issues related to Catholic faith, morality, eucharistic liturgy, the ritual of the sacraments, Christian community, and the Church's administrative structure. For our purposes it was not until this council that a universalist position on the universal salvific will of God became strongly supported. Here the universal salvific will of God became the focus. In brief, the Second Vatican Council affirmed that non-Christians could be saved; that God desires all people to be saved; that God knows and loves all people; that there are elements of truth in other religions; and that the Church continues to be an instrument of salvation. There has never been a council that has spoken so positively about other religions. The council boasts of a God who "with loving concern" is "making preparation for the salvation of the whole human race."[1] In the prologue of the Dogmatic Constitution on Divine Revelation, *Dei Verbum*, the council insists that "it wants the whole world to hear the summons of salvation, so that through hearing it may believe, through belief it may hope, through hope it may come to love."[2] God's desire to transmit salvation to all generations is a recurrent theme in this council. We hear of God's activity in the history of revelation and salvation before the Christ-event, as from the very beginning "creation was already oriented toward salvation."[3] Hence, the council explains how salvation is announced through the Church.

The documents of the council uphold the two truth claims, namely, the universal salvific will of God and the universality and particularity of Jesus Christ as Savior. The teaching of the official documents leading up to the council had focused more heavily on the necessity of explicit faith in Jesus Christ as Savior and the mediation of the Church. It seemed as though these beliefs had greater prominence than the belief in the universal salvific will of God.

While the possibility of salvation outside the Church had been affirmed by official teaching before this council, the Second Vatican Council further develops this discussion. The documents of this council, then, affirm the possibility of salvation of people outside the Church and the Church's acknowledgment of the values and truths found in the religions of the world. While this chapter considers several key documents, the main texts to be examined, in the order of publication by the council, are the constitution *Lumen Gentium*, the declaration *Nostra Aetate*, and the decree *Ad Gentes*. These three documents should be considered together as they contain teachings influenced by the council's desire to communicate better its teaching on the universal salvific will of God and the religions of the world. Hence, they represent a key development in the teaching of the Church since the early centuries.

These documents address the individual salvation of members of other religions and the role their religions play in their salvation. They mark a shift away from what has been called the replacement theory, with Christianity as the ultimate replacement of all religions, to a fulfillment theory, where other religions are seen as stepping stones to or preparation for Christianity. The council recognized supernatural grace-filled elements in the religions of the world. However, this shift was in development several years before the council as theologians attempted to articulate ways in which God extended the gift of salvation to members of other religions. Hence, before we enter into discussion with the documents of the council it is helpful to consider briefly the contributions made by some scholars, most notably that of Karl Rahner, as his contributions had some influence on the views of the council.

Preconciliar Influences

Karl Rahner was a German Jesuit who contributed much to the discussion of the Church's understanding of religions. In 1961, he began to look at the theology of religions. According to Rahner, God offers the possibility of salvation to all people. However, this salvation is mediated through the person of Jesus Christ. For Rahner, Christianity understands itself "as the absolute religion" intended for all people, "which cannot recognize any other religion, beside itself as of equal right."[4] Moreover, the salvation offered through Christianity is a salvation intended for all people. In other words, Christianity holds a unique place in the history of salvation. Faith, for Rahner, marks a response to God, who offers the revelation necessary to attain salvation. God, he affirms, desires to save all people and will offer the grace and means necessary to enable every person to be saved. God's offered grace, then, is part of our historical human nature; however, it remains the grace of Christ. Rahner refers to this mystery as the "supernatural existential." Our nature is graced and enabled to respond to God's call of salvation. This suggests that all people are invited to be saved. Jesus, however, is the cause of this salvation. Jesus is the "absolute savior"[5] and the sign that God is with us. Christ is in all persons, inviting them through grace to embrace salvation. However, Rahner acknowledges that there are millions of people who do not know Jesus. These people, he posits, can still receive God's grace and be led to Christ whether they know it or not. He names these people "anonymous Christians."[6]

"Anonymous Christianity" refers to the hidden and unknown mystery of Christ that is at work in other religions. It is this mystery that, for Rahner, makes salvation possible for members of other religions. He affirms that the universal salvific will of God is "really operative in the world."[7] "Anonymous Christianity" implies that revelation and faith are possible everywhere and "hence throughout the whole length and breadth of the history of the human race."[8] This allows him to conclude that Christ is "present and operative"[9] in members of other religious traditions "in and through his Spirit."[10] Non-Christian religions, then,

> contain elements of natural knowledge of God, more-over,…supernatural elements arising out of the grace which is given to people as a gratuitous gift on account of Christ. For this reason a non-Christian religion can be recognized as a lawful religion…it is *a priori* quite possible to suppose that there are supernatural grace-filled elements in non-Christian religions.[11]

In other words, Rahner posits that all people are exposed to elements of the divine within their own religious traditions—an insight to be borrowed in the documents of the Second Vatican Council. However, the council did not go as far as Rahner in referring to other believers as "anonymous Christians," as this may have led to the conclusion that other religions may be "ways of salvation." Nevertheless, the council did go on to express the possibility of salvation for members of other religions; however, it is salvation in Christ. In this way Rahner continued to be an influence in the consideration of views toward other religions.

Rahner, however, is not the only theologian to influence the documents of the Second Vatican Council. It is helpful to briefly consider Henri de Lubac, who was a proponent of the fulfillment theory, which went on to have an impact on the council.[12] According to the fulfillment theory,

> the mystery of Christ reaches the members of other religious traditions as the divine response to the human aspiration for union with the Divine, but the religious traditions themselves play no role in this mystery of salvation.[13]

While other religions serve as a preparation for salvation, Christianity remains the fulfillment of salvation. de Lubac writes:

> Christianity brought into the world something absolutely new. Its concept of salvation is not only original in relation to that of the religions that surrounded its birth; it constitutes a unique event in the religious history of humankind…In this universal symphony (of religions) Christianity alone affirms, at once and indissolubly, a transcendent destiny of the human person and for the whole of humankind a common destiny. For this destiny the entire history of the world is a preparation. From the first creation down to the final consummation…a unique divine project is being fulfilled.[14]

Viewing other religions as preparation for Christianity is another insight to be taken up by the council. Christianity is the one universal religion intended for all people. Hence, for de Lubac, other religions serve as stepping stones to Christianity. Christianity has a message for all people and offers the fulfillment of salvation. While de Lubac acknowledges salvation outside Christianity, this salvation does not take place without Christ or apart from him. He was able to see the mysterious presence of Jesus Christ in other religions and his contributions, together with those of Rahner and other theologians, inspired the Second Vatican Council to view other religions with greater openness. Let us consider the documents of this council and see what each document has to say about the mystery of the salvific will of God and its treatment of members of other religions.

The Documents of the Second Vatican Council on Salvation and Other Religious Traditions

LUMEN GENTIUM: THE CHURCH CALLS ALL PEOPLE TO EXPERIENCE SALVATION

The first document to be published that deals with salvation outside the Church is the Dogmatic Constitution on the Church, or *Lumen Gentium.* This document is key to our discussion, as it affirms the Church's call to all people to experience salvation in Christ. The constitution begins with an affirmation of God's love for humanity and with the description of Christ as the light of humanity. Moreover, the Church is viewed as the sacrament of salvation.[15] However, the Church consists of a new people of God[16] in Christ: "the universal Church is to be seen to be a people brought into unity from the unity of the Father, the Son and the Holy Spirit."[17]

The Church is to be a sight of what God wills to offer the world: salvation with Christ. Hence the Church, as a sign of salvation, calls all people to experience salvation in Christ: "All men are called to this union with Christ, who is the light of the world, from whom we go forth, through whom we live, and towards whom our whole life is directed."[18] While the constitution affirms that "it is through Christ's Catholic Church alone, which is the all-embracing means of salvation, that the fullness of the means of salvation can be found,"[19] it does acknowledge that truth and goodness found in other religions are to be considered as "preparation for the Gospel"[20] and that they are "oriented toward" their fulfillment in Christ and the Church.[21] These views are similar to the insights of Rahner and de Lubac. The constitution goes on to speak of different ways in which members of other religions are oriented to the Church. Those who have not received the gospel "are related to the People of God in various ways."[22]

Lumen Gentium refers first to Jews and Muslims:

> There is, first, that people to which the covenants and promises were made, and from which Christ was born according to the flesh (cf. Rom. 9:4–5): in view of the divine choice, they are a people most dear for the sake of the fathers, for the gifts of God are without repentance (cf. Rom. 11:29). But the plan of salvation also includes those who acknowledge the Creator, in the first place amongst whom are the Moslems: these profess to hold the faith of Abraham, and together with us they adore the one, merciful God, mankind's judge on the last day.[23]

The constitution goes on to acknowledge God's closeness to members of non-monotheistic religions:

> Nor is God remote from those who in shadows and images seek the unknown God, since he gives to all men life and breath in all things (cf. Acts. 17:25–28), and since the Savior wills all men to be saved (cf. 1 Tim. 2:4). Those who through no fault of their own, do not know the Gospel of Christ or his Church, but who nevertheless seek God with a sincere heart, and, moved by grace, try in their actions to do his will as they know it through the dictates of their conscience—those too may achieve eternal salvation. Nor shall divine providence deny the assistance necessary for salvation to those who, without any fault of theirs, have not yet arrived at an explicit knowledge of God, and who, not without grace, strive to lead a good life. Whatever truth or good is found amongst them is considered by the Church to be a preparation for the Gospel and given by him who enlightens all men that they may at length have life.[24]

Hence, salvation is extended to members of other monotheistic religions as well as to people who in "shadows and images seek the unknown God," since the saving presence of God—God's grace—is close to them. The constitution reaffirms the Church's teaching on inculpable ignorance and acknowledges people's genuine desire to do God's will "as they know it through the dictates of their conscience." Thus God's desire to save all people is not limited by different religious beliefs because "the one goodness of God is radiated in different ways among his creatures."[25] Moreover, the truth and good found in these religions are to be considered as "preparation for the Gospel." The Church attributes a positive value to individual people's desire to seek truth and God. However, some people "have exchanged the truth of God for a lie and served the world rather than the Creator (cf. Rom. 1:21, 25)."[26] It is for this reason that the Church's mission consists of preaching the gospel of salvation to all people.[27] Hence the Church, in *Lumen Gentium*, acknowledges not only the rightful dispositions of individual persons, but it affirms the goodness found in these religious traditions; however, it belongs to the mission of the Church to bring these religions to fulfillment through the hearing of the gospel. The rites and customs of these religions can be "purified, raised up, and perfected" through the work of the Holy Spirit. It is here that the fulfillment theory is played out. Members of these religions are "oriented to" the mystical body of Christ. The 1965 Declaration on the Relation of the Church to Non-Christian Religions, or *Nostra Aetate*, however, presents a different approach to the religions of the world. The emphasis in this document is not the orientation of members of other religions toward the Church, but rather on the promotion of fellowship among the religions.

NOSTRA AETATE: DIALOGUE, COLLABORATION, AND FELLOWSHIP

Once again, in this declaration, the Church emphasizes Christ's redemptive activity in the world. While the declaration considers the impact of exploration, mass communication, travel, and the stronger ties between different cultures, it teaches that we "all share a common destiny, namely God."[28] As regards Hinduism and Buddhism, the Church

> rejects nothing of what is true and holy in these religions. She has a high regard for the manner of life and conduct, the precepts and doctrines which, although differing in many ways from her own teaching, nevertheless reflect a ray of light of that truth which enlightens all men.[29]

It goes on to note that it has a "high regard for the Muslims" and while the Church acknowledges the strained relationship between the two religions, it calls for healing and reconciliation, for "mutual understanding" and the working together to promote "peace, liberty, social justice and moral values."[30] Next, the declaration considers the close ties between Christianity and Judaism.

What is significant is that the council affirms that God's desire to save people predates Christianity. The gift of salvation extends back to the patriarchs.[31] Thus, Jews are saved through their own covenant[32] and Christians are called to remember that the Jewish people were the first to embrace Jesus. Hence, there is no mention of converting Jews to Christianity. This document, then, marks a large step forward in Jewish-Christian relations and relating God's offer of salvation to all people. The declaration affirms that the universal salvific will of God transcends all barriers. Thus, the above two documents emphasize the presence of grace (LG) and of truth and goodness in other religions (NA), and the notion of fulfillment is addressed (LG). The idea of fulfillment is included in the Decree on the Mission Activity of the Church, or *Ad Gentes*. According to this decree, other religions find their fulfillment in the gospel.

Ad Gentes was completed on December 7, 1965. The preface introduces the main theme of the document: the Church has been "divinely sent to the nations, that she might be 'the universal sacrament of salvation.'"[33] While *Lumen Gentium* begins with the declaration that "Christ is the light of all nations,"[34] *Ad Gentes* begins with the affirmation that "the Church has been divinely sent to all nations."[35] The decree goes on to declare that the Church "by its very nature" is missionary.[36] The word of God is to be preached throughout the world so that the kingdom of God can be "proclaimed and renewed."[37] The salvation of the world, accomplished through Jesus Christ, continues to be proclaimed to all people:

> This universal plan for salvation of mankind is not carried out solely in secret manner, as it were, in the minds of men, nor by the efforts, even religious, through which they in many ways seek God in an attempt to touch him and find him, although God is not far away from any of us...; their efforts need to be enlightened and corrected, although in the loving providence of God they may lead one to the true God and be a preparation for the Gospel...Now, what was once preached by the Lord, or fulfilled in him for the salvation of mankind, must be proclaimed and spread to the ends of the earth..., starting from Jerusalem (cf. Lk. 24:27), so that what was accomplished for the salvation of all men may, in the course of time, achieve its universal effect.[38]

Hence, the religions of the world can be used as a "preparation for the Gospel"; however, the gospel must continue to be proclaimed for the salvation of all people. Jesus set up "the apostolic ministry" and sent the Holy Spirit for the "fulfillment of the work of salvation."[39] Thus, "Christ sent the Holy Spirit from the Father to exercise inwardly his saving influence, and to promote the spread of the Church. Without doubt, the Holy Spirit was at work in the world before Christ was glorified."[40] While the council does not offer a developed theology of the Spirit, it represents the beginning of a new appreciation for the work of the Spirit in the religions of the world.

While the Church "possesses the fullness of the means of salvation" it recognizes "elements of truth and grace"[41] in other religions. Moreover, Christians are called to acknowledge "seeds of the Word which lie hidden"[42] in other religions. "A secret presence of God"[43] found in these "elements of truth and grace" helps draw people closer to God. While the Catholic Church "rejects nothing that is true and holy in these religions,"[44] *Ad Gentes* concludes that these "elements of truth and grace" are "perfected for the glory of God"[45] by the Church. Christians, then, are called to "sincere and patient dialogue" so that they might learn "of the riches which a generous God has distributed among the nations. They must at the same time endeavor to illuminate these riches with the light of the Gospel, set them free, and bring them once more under the dominion of God the savior."[46] However, another document, issued in the same year as *Ad Gentes*, the Declaration on Religious Freedom, *Dignitatis Humanae*, cautions against engaging in dialogue or missionary activity that imposes on religious freedom and frustrates one's search for truth.

Dignitatis Humanae begins by declaring that people can be saved by serving God.[47] Furthermore, it affirms that "the human person has a right to religious freedom,"[48] and has a duty to follow the truth. Moreover, every person has the right to follow his conscience:

> It is through conscience that man sees and recognizes the demands of the divine law. He is bound to follow his conscience faithfully in all his activity so that he may come to God, who is his last end. Therefore, he must not be forced to act contrary to his conscience. Nor must he be prevented from acting according to his conscience, especially in religious matters.[49]

Thus, Christians and members of other religious traditions have the right to religious freedom, to pursue the truth, and to follow their conscience.

Ad Gentes supports mission work while *Dignitatis Humanae* affirms the necessity of religious freedom. The council, then, expressed respect and concern for the freedom and dignity of the individual. Nevertheless, *Ad Gentes* calls for continued proclamation. While God's plan for salvation includes people regardless of religious affiliation, the missionary task of the Church is to continue to preach the gospel in preparation for Christ's second coming.[50] The human race seeks God through various religions; however, the decree affirms that Jesus brings salvation to the world, as he is the only Savior.[51]

Referring to Mark 16:16,[52] the decree supports missionary work and the necessity of the Church. However, the document makes reference to the issues of inculpable and culpable ignorance:

> Hence those cannot be saved, who, knowing that the Catholic Church was founded through Jesus Christ, by God, as something necessary, still refuse to enter it, or to remain in it. So, although in ways known to himself God can lead those who, through no fault of their own, are ignorant of the Gospel to that faith without which it is impossible to please him (Heb. 11:6), the Church, nevertheless, still has the obligation and also the sacred right to evangelize. And so, today as always, missionary activity retains its full force and necessity.[53]

Hence, those people who are aware of the Church, and see its necessity, but do not respond faithfully, cannot be saved. On the other hand, those who "through no fault of their own" do not know Christ can still be saved through faith in God. Nevertheless, the gospel message must still be extended to all people. The decree views non-Christian religions as "preparation for the Gospel"[54]; therefore, missionaries can build on such a foundation as they transmit the gospel to non-Christians.

In this decree it is the salvific will of God that drives missionary activity:

> The reason for missionary activity lies in the will of God,
> "who wishes all men to be saved and to come to the knowledge of the truth. For there is one God and one mediator
> between God and men, himself a man Jesus Christ, who
> gave himself as a ransom for all" (1 Tim. 2:4–5), "neither is
> there salvation in any other" (Acts 4:12).[55]

Here we have two key claims reaffirmed: the universal salvific
will of God and the particularity of Jesus Christ as Savior of all
people. While God's desire to save is limitless and transcends
race, culture, and creed, missionary activity is still needed.

Ultimately, salvation remains mystical and mysterious.
Nonetheless, it was refreshing to read in these three documents that
God is working salvifically in the religions of the world. The
Church has developed and advanced its teaching on the universal
salvific will of God. Its view of salvation has shifted from a spirit of
exclusivity to one of inclusivity. However, in one more document,
the 1965 Pastoral Constitution on the Church in the Modern World,
Gaudium et Spes, Jesus' place in salvation history is made clear.

Gaudium et Spes, rooted in *Lumen Gentium*, is one of the most
quoted of the council's documents. Similar in tone to the above three
documents, it recognizes that in the religions there are "precious
things, both religious and human,"[56] that salvation is possible outside the visible boundaries of the Church,[57] and that the salvation
offered through Christ applies not only to Christians but to all
people who do God's will and are open to the grace of Christ that is
secretly present in their hearts:

> All this holds true not only for Christians only but for all men
> of good will in whose hearts grace is active invisibly. For
> since Christ died for all, and since all men are in fact called to
> one and the same destiny, which is divine, we must hold that

the Holy Spirit offers to all the possibility of being made
partners, in a way known to God, in the paschal mystery.[58]

The Holy Spirit, then, connects members of other religions
to the paschal mystery. Jesus Christ, affirms the council, is central
to this process of fulfillment, renewal, and salvation.[59] All people
are called to fulfillment and salvation, and this calling is inclusive
as is the universal salvific will of God. The above documents
express that the council held strong to three claims, namely, the
universal salvific will of God (LG 2, 3, 26; AG 7), Jesus as mediator of salvation (GS 10, 45), and the necessity of the Church (LG
1, 9, 48; GS 42, 45; AG 1, 5). While the council presented these
teachings with some variations in the key documents addressed in
this chapter, it left room for discussion and clarification. Theologians and magisterial documents have continued to examine the
salvific significance of other religions. Official postconciliar documents, however, are marked by a significant tension with regard
to the issue of whether the council meant to assign a positive role
for the other religions.

The Pontificate of John Paul II

The teaching of the Second Vatican Council has left room
for theologians and recent magisterial documents to develop further teaching on the universal salvific will of God and how it is
communicated in the religions of the world. While there remains
room for development, the documents of the council displayed a
positive attitude toward dialogue with the religions of the world.
The language of the "dialogue of salvation" put forward by Paul
VI in the 1964 encyclical *Ecclesiam Suam* encouraged all people
to reconsider the universal salvific will of God in light of evangelization and dialogue:

The dialogue of salvation was opened spontaneously on the
initiative of God...The dialogue of salvation began with

charity, with the divine goodness: "God so loved the world as to give His only begotten Son..." The dialogue of salvation did not physically force anyone to accept it; it was a tremendous appeal of love which, although placing a vast responsibility on those toward whom it was directed, nevertheless left them free to respond to it or to reject it...The dialogue of salvation was made accessible to all; it was destined for all without distinction; in like manner our own dialogue should be potentially universal, i.e. all embracing and capable of including all, excepting only one who would either absolutely reject it or insincerely pretend to accept it. (ES 72, 73, 75, 76)

This "dialogue of salvation" went on to be included in the teaching of John Paul II and the Secretariat for Non-Christian Religions. John Paul II emphasizes the universal action of the Holy Spirit in the religions of the world as he strives to stay close to the council's teaching on the universal salvific will.

The contribution of John Paul II was influenced by his interest in, and respect for, religious diversity. His interest in the religions of the world impacted his theology of salvation. He used a theology of the Holy Spirit in his attempt to explain God's activity in the religions of the world. Salvation, for John Paul II, originates in God, is accomplished in Jesus Christ, and continues to be mediated by the Holy Spirit.

Step Five: The Role of the Holy Spirit in Salvation

Redemptor Hominis

In the first half of his papacy, John Paul II advanced the teaching of the Second Vatican Council through his theology of the Holy Spirit. While *Ad Gentes* (4) and *Gaudium et Spes* (22) referred to the role of the Spirit in the world, this pope's teaching went on to develop a theology of the Spirit with respect to the religions of the world. In his first encyclical (1979), The Redeemer of Man, *Redemptor Hominis*, he mentions the "one Spirit of truth" that unites all religions.[60] In this encyclical he demonstrates an appreciation for members of other religions. He desires to engage in dialogue with the religions of the world. The beliefs of those who follow other religions he recognizes as an "effect of the Spirit of truth operating outside the visible confines of the Mystical Body."[61] The Holy Spirit, for John Paul II, plays a significant role in his theology of salvation. He acknowledges the presence and activity of the Holy Spirit in the religions of the world.

John Paul II calls Christians to acknowledge truths in other religions. These truths are made known by the same Spirit that enlightens Christians.[62] This Spirit, then, which "blows where it wills,"[63] is present in all authentic prayer regardless of religious affiliation. This theme continued to be articulated in the Assisi prayer meeting held on October 27, 1986, where John Paul II called the people of the world to be "aware of the common origin and common destiny of humanity." In the same year he produced another encyclical on the Holy Spirit, On the Holy Spirit in the Life of the Church and the World, *Dominum et Vivificantem*, in which he examines the Spirit's activity in the world beyond the visible confines of the Church. This encyclical, dated on the feast of Pentecost, May 18, 1986, was issued with the intent to challenge the materialism that enslaves so many people. The pope proclaims the gift of the Spirit and calls people to conversion and closeness to God.

Dominum et Vivificantem

John Paul II calls for a proper appreciation of the universal action of the Holy Spirit that begins before the Christ-event:

> We cannot limit ourselves to the 2,000 years which have passed since the birth of Christ. We need to go further back, to embrace the whole of the action of the Holy Spirit even

before Christ—from the beginning throughout the world and especially in the economy of the old covenant. For this action has been exercised at every place and at every time, indeed, in every individual, according to the eternal plan of salvation whereby this action was to be closely linked with the mystery of the incarnation and redemption, which in turn exercised its influence on those who believed in the future coming of Christ...But we need to look further and go further afield knowing that the "wind blows where it wills," according to the image used by Jesus in his conversation with Nicodemus. The Second Vatican Council, centred primarily on the theme of the church, reminds us of the Holy Spirit's activity also "outside the visible body of the church." The council speaks precisely of "all people of good will in whose hearts grace works in an unseen way. For, since Christ died for all, and since the ultimate vocation of man is in fact one, and divine, we ought to believe that the Holy Spirit in a manner known only to God offers to every man the possibility of being associated with this paschal mystery."[64]

The Holy Spirit, then, makes salvation possible for members of other religious traditions. In *Dominum et Vivificantem* John Paul II develops the thought of the Second Vatican Council. The Spirit is at work in religious traditions worldwide, bringing salvation to their adherents.

Redemptoris Missio

In a subsequent encyclical, On the Permanent Validity of the Church's Missionary Mandate, *Redemptoris Missio*, issued on the twenty-fifth anniversary of *Ad Gentes* in 1990, John Paul II continues his inclusive view of the Spirit when he states that the Spirit's activity is not limited to individuals; it works in communities and religions.[65] However, while the gift of salvation is offered to all people as it is mediated through the activity of the

Holy Spirit, it is, for the pope, always salvation in Christ.[66] John
Paul II writes:

> While acknowledging that God loves all people and grants
> them the possibility of being saved (cf. 1 Tim. 2:4; LG 14–17;
> AG 3), the Church believes that God has established Christ as
> the one mediator and that she herself has been established as
> the universal sacrament of salvation (LG 48; GS 43; AG 7, 21).
>   It is necessary to keep these two truths together, namely, the
> real possibility of salvation in Christ for all mankind and the
> necessity of the Church for salvation. Both these truths help us
> to understand the one mystery of salvation, so that we can
> come to know God's mercy and our own responsibility. Salva-
> tion which always remains a gift of the Spirit, requires man's
> cooperation, both to save himself and to save others. This is
> God's will.[67]

Hence, the Church remains Christ's "co-worker in the salvation
of the world," and each person must respond to and cooperate
with God's will. Nevertheless, the salvation accomplished in
Christ is offered to all through the activity of the Spirit since it is a
"gift of the Spirit" to the people of the world. The Spirit brings
this gift to all people, even to those who do not know Christ:

> The universality of salvation means that it is granted not
> only to those who explicitly believe in Christ and have
> entered the Church. Since salvation is offered to all, it must
> be made concretely available to all. But it is clear that today,
> as in the past, many people do not have the opportunity to
> come to know or accept the Gospel revelation or to enter the
> Church. The social and cultural conditions in which they
> live do not permit this and frequently they have been
> brought up in other religious traditions. For such people sal-
> vation in Christ is accessible by virtue of a grace which,
> while having a mysterious relationship to the Church, does
> not make them formally part of the Church but enlightens
> them in a way which is accommodated in their spiritual and

material situation. This grace comes from Christ; it is the result of his sacrifice and is communicated by the Holy Spirit. It enables each person to attain salvation through his or her free cooperation.[68]

Thus, the Spirit continues Christ's desire to bring "integral salvation, one which embraces the whole person and all mankind."[69] Even for those who are "brought up in other religious traditions," the Spirit will work within their "spiritual condition." While John Paul II does not go as far to say that other religions are themselves "mediations" of salvation, he does speak of participated forms of mediation:

> Although participated forms of mediation of different kinds and degrees are not excluded, they acquire meaning and value only from Christ's own mediation, and they cannot be understood as parallel or complementary to his.[70]

It seems as though John Paul II is acknowledging the salvific function of other religions, albeit inferior to Christ's unique mediation. However, this ambiguity has led some to think that the pope is implying that other religions may be ways of salvation. While John Paul II will not go as far as to declare the religions as "ways of salvation," his pneumatology inspires him to appreciate those sacred elements found in the religions of the world that move their members toward the gift of salvation. It is his appreciation for the work of the Holy Spirit that has influenced his approach to members of other religions.[71]

To this point, John Paul II has built upon the positive insights of the Second Vatican Council. He develops the insight on the Holy Spirit that appears briefly, with no further development, in *Gaudium et Spes* (22). In contrast, John Paul II uses the universal action of the Holy Spirit as a theme in his discussion of the religions of the world. Recall his words that the Spirit continues the work of salvation by communicating the grace needed for "integral salvation" to those who are "brought up in other religious traditions." However, he will not compromise the teaching that Jesus is the universal Savior nor that the Church plays a mediatory role in the salvation of humanity. Members of other religions can be saved, but always through the grace of Christ. John Paul II considers "participated forms of mediations" ways in which members of other religious traditions participate in Christ's mediation. It seems as though the pope is implying that all mediation between God and people is a participation in Christ's mediation, thus receiving "meaning and value only from Christ's own mediation." While he does not exclude "participated forms of mediation," he does not explicitly declare that religions can be "mediations" of salvation for their members.

Early in *Redemptoris Missio* John Paul II asks: "Is it not possible to attain salvation in any religion?" While he does not answer this question clearly or in depth, he does acknowledge that the religions of the world play a role in the salvation of their adherents. They may not be "parallel or complementary" to the mediation of Christ, but, nevertheless, he declares that they contribute to the salvation of people. His understanding of the role other religions play in communicating the universal salvific will of God is one that needs to be explored further. Before the publication of *Redemptoris Missio*, John Paul II found himself addressing the Secretariat for Non-Christians and asking the very questions that he himself had attempted to answer:

> There remain many questions which we have to develop and articulate more clearly. How does God work in the lives of peoples of different religions? How does his saving activity in Jesus Christ effectively extend to those who have not professed faith in him? In coming years, these questions and related ones will become more and more important for the Church in a pluralistic world, and pastors with the collaboration of experienced theologians, must direct their studious attention to them.[72]

Of interest here is that this secretariat to whom these questions are addressed, which in 1988 was renamed the Pontifical

Council for Interreligious Dialogue by John Paul II, joined together with the Congregation for the Evangelization of Peoples and issued a document entitled *Dialogue and Proclamation* in 1991 on the twenty-fifth anniversary of *Nostra Aetate* that set out to explore the meaning and purpose of interreligious dialogue and the proclamation of Jesus Christ. In other words, this document addresses the very questions posed by John Paul II five years earlier. This document is relevant to our discussion, as it complements *Redemptoris Missio* and offers a fuller response to the question of the mediatory role of the religions in the universal salvific will of God. While this document does not hold the same authority as the encyclicals of John Paul II, it represents and is rooted in his desire to understand better the relationship between interreligious dialogue and proclamation of the gospel. Moreover, it goes beyond what is taught in the encyclical. Of interest here is how the document presents its view on the universal salvific will of God and how it addresses the teaching of the encyclical *Redemptoris Missio.*

Clarifying the Salvific Function of Other Religious Traditions

Dialogue and Proclamation

From the beginning, the jointly authored document states that dialogue and proclamation are part of the Church's evangelizing mission.[73] Further, "they are both oriented toward the communication of salvific truth."[74] Interreligious dialogue, then, and proclamation are to be used to communicate a "dialogue of salvation."[75] While they differ in purpose, they are to be used to communicate the truth of God. This "salvific truth," as was previously stated by the Second Vatican Council and John Paul II, is mediated by the Holy Spirit.[76] What is key here is that in their interpretation of the documents of the Second Vatican Council, the authors of this document affirm that elements in the religions of the world "play a providential role in the divine economy of salvation."[77]

John Paul II, in *Redemptoris Missio*, acknowledged "participated mediations" and made note of a certain type of contribution, albeit inferior to the mediation of Jesus Christ. This document, however, begins with a more generous description of the role of religions in communicating the universal salvific will of God. Jesus Christ remains the source of salvation, but "the mystery of salvation reaches out to them (members of other religions), in a way known to God through the invisible action of the Spirit of Christ."[78] Building on and developing the views of the council, the document declares that even while people may not recognize Jesus as their Savior, "it will be in sincere practice of what is good in their own traditions and by following the dictates of their conscience that the members of other religions respond positively to God's invitation and receive salvation in Jesus Christ."[79]

It is this affirmation that marks a big step beyond both the teaching of the council and of John Paul II. These statements suggest that members of other religions can be saved through "the sincere practice of what is good in their own traditions." This surely assigns a greater role to their religions than that which was previously assigned by John Paul II in *Redemptoris Missio*. It also says more than respecting "whatever is good…in the rites and customs proper to various peoples."[80] Instead, it cautiously suggests that God's channels of grace are operative in the beliefs and practices of other religions. Nevertheless, the document continuously affirms that members of other religions are saved by Jesus Christ[81] and that the Church is the "universal sacrament of salvation."[82]

This document, then, proposes a "dialogue of salvation" and the role of the Church as the "sign and instrument of the divine plan of salvation"[83] and the truth that "God, in an age-long dialogue, has offered and continues to offer salvation to humankind. In faithfulness to the divine initiative, the Church too must enter into a dialogue of salvation with all men and women."[84] It is through this dialogue that Christians may learn from the positive values found in other religions. This document acknowledges that the universal salvific will of God is made known implicitly through dialogue and explicitly through proclamation. These two activities are linked since they are both part of the Church's evangelizing mission. *Dialogue and Proclamation*, then, affirms the teachings of the council and John Paul II, but goes beyond their insights and recognizes that the religions of the world play an important role in communicating the universal salvific will of God. This document continues to note that members of other religious traditions can be saved in their own traditions. Another document that follows this positive approach is the 1997 statement of the International Theological Commission, *Christianity and the World Religions*.

Christianity and the World Religions

The authors of *Christianity and the World Religions* begin their discussion by noting that Christians, "and specifically the Catholic Church, must try to clarify how religions are to be evaluated theologically."[85] To this end the document asks: "Do religions mediate salvation to their members?" and, if so, "Are such mediations of salvation autonomous or do they convey the salvation of Jesus Christ?" While the question as to whether members of other religions can be saved has been answered, these new questions explore ways in which the universal salvific will is played out in the religions of the world.

This document reaffirms the teaching of past documents that declare "there is only one God and one plan of salvation, which is the same for all humanity." Moreover, "the expressions of religion are interconnected and mutually complementary."[86] Ultimately, God desires all people to be saved and interreligious dialogue is to be based on the claim that we all have our common origin in God and we are created in the image and likeness of God. For Christians, however, dialogue is based on "their common destiny which is the fullness of life in God, or on the single divine plan of salvation through Jesus Christ, or on the active presence of the divine Spirit among the followers of other religious traditions."[87] Thus, God's salvific action is accomplished in Jesus Christ and works through all religions by the universal action of the Holy Spirit. The document asks: "Could one not conceive of the person and salvific action of God starting from other mediators as well as Jesus Christ?" In response to this question the document goes on to explain the four phases of God's universal salvific action.

This section of the document begins with the affirmation that there is a divine plan of salvation for all humanity. This plan is not limited by race or religion. "The God who wishes to save all is the Father of our Lord Jesus Christ."[88] God's plan of salvation preceded the creation of the world "and is realized with the sending of Jesus into the world, proof of the infinite love and tenderness which the Father has for humanity."[89] The salvation, then, that God offers to all nations is Jesus himself. Hence, God initiates salvation, then the "work of salvation is realized by Christ."[90] Thus, even before Jesus is Savior, God is Savior—God the Savior desires that all people know of God's plan to save them. The salvific will of God, then, has been intended since the creation of the world. God's initiative to offer salvation to all people is evident in the Hebrew scriptures and finds its fulfillment in Jesus Christ. Here we enter the second phase of God's universal salvific action, namely, the unique mediation of Jesus.

Immediately, in this section, the document claims that only in Jesus is God's salvific plan realized. It quotes Acts 4:12, which declares that "there is no other name under heaven given among mortals by which we must be saved." However, it goes on to confirm the "universality of the saving work of Jesus" that is offered to all people. Moreover, Jesus' unique mediation is connected to the universal salvific will of God: "There is one God and there is one mediator between God and men, the man Jesus Christ who gave himself as a ransom for all" (1 Tim 2:5–6). "The uniqueness of the mediator corresponds to the uniqueness of God, who

desires the salvation of all."[91] The commission continues to refer
to the New Testament as it notes the link between salvation and
the "redemptive work of Christ Jesus, the only mediator." Hence,
in response to the question "Could one not conceive of the person
and salvific action of God starting from other mediators as well as
Jesus Christ?" the commission states: "The New Testament message is not compatible with any limiting of the salvific will of
God, or with admitting any mediations parallel to that of Jesus or
with attributing this universal mediation to the eternal Logos in
isolation from Jesus."[92] Hence, all salvific action is related to
Jesus Christ:

> Other possibilities of salvific "mediation" cannot be seen in
> isolation from the man Jesus, the only mediator. It will be
> more difficult to determine how human beings who do not
> know Jesus and other religions are related to Jesus. Mention
> should be made of the mysterious ways of the Spirit, who
> gives to all the possibility of being associated with the
> paschal mystery (*Gaudium et Spes* 22) and whose work can-
> not be without reference to Christ (*Redemptoris Missio* 29).
> The question of the salvific value of religions as such must
> be situated in the context of the universal active presence of
> the Spirit of Christ.[93]

While it is clear here that the commission affirms Jesus as
the only mediator, it seems as though it may be suggesting that
there are "other possibilities of salvific 'mediation.'" Does this
mean that there are other inferior mediations that can be related to
the ultimate mediation of Jesus Christ? Perhaps we will find the
answer in the commission's examination of the next phase of
God's universal salvific plan: the universality of the Holy Spirit.

To begin, the universal salvific activity of the Spirit must be
understood as related to the universal salvific activity of Christ.[94]
The commission begins its discussion of the Holy Spirit with the
affirmation that "the work of the Holy Spirit is already found in
creation. The Old Testament shows us the Spirit of God hovering

over the waters (Gn. 1:2). And the book of Wisdom (1:7) points out that 'the spirit of the Lord has filled the world, and that which holds all things together knows what is said.'" The commission goes on to state that the universal presence of the Holy Spirit makes salvation possible for members of other religious traditions. Jesus "works in the hearts of men through the Holy Spirit and...it is the same Spirit who distributes the seeds of the word present in the rites and religions."[95]

The religions of the world, the commission notes, challenge the Church because "they stimulate her to recognize the signs of the presence of Christ and the action of the Spirit."[96] It is this recognition of the presence of the Spirit of Christ in the religions of the world that leads the commission to consider the possibility that these religions "exercise as such a certain salvific function." While the commission, earlier in the document, noted that the question as to whether the religions "as such can have a salvific value" remained open, it seems to have answered it soon after:

> Given this explicit recognition of the presence of the Spirit of Christ in the religions, one cannot exclude the possibility that they exercise as such a certain salvific function.[97]

The commission goes on to declare that these religions can "help men achieve their ultimate end." The commission continues:

> It would be difficult to think that what the Holy Spirit works in the hearts of men taken as individuals would have salvific value and not think that what the Holy Spirit works in the religions and cultures would not have such value...The religions can be carriers of saving truth only insofar as they raise men to true love.[98]

While the commission does not go as far to say that other religions are "ways of salvation" equal to the way of Jesus, it does note that "they exercise a certain salvific function." The reason for this can be found in the commission's discussion of the final phase of God's universal salvific plan: "The Church, the Universal Sacrament of Salvation."

The commission connects the religions to the Church through the activity of the Spirit: "In the religions the same Spirit who guides the Church is at work."[99] It contends that, while the Spirit is universally present in the religions, the presence of the Spirit in the Church is special and beyond comparison. This is due to the "gaps" found in the religions: "Although one cannot exclude the salvific value of the religions, this does not mean that everything in them is salvific."[100] Nevertheless, the commission does acknowledge the role played by the religions of the world in communicating and accepting the universal salvific will of God.

One can safely conclude that the commission affirms God's desire to save all people; that salvation extends beyond the visible boundaries of the Church; that the Holy Spirit is present in the religions of the world, calling their members forth to receive the salvation initiated by God and accomplished by Jesus Christ; and that God will use these religions as a "means" of helping their followers achieve salvation. While their function is inferior to the function of the Church, they, nevertheless, "exercise a certain salvific function." This document, then, builds upon the pneumatology of John Paul II and the Second Vatican Council and challenges Christians to consider the salvific value found in the religions of the world. The universal salvific will of God, then, is communicated through four phases and these religions are part of this process. The next official document to be considered is the most controversial of the group. *Dominus Iesus* is the most recent magisterial document to tackle ecumenical and interreligious issues related to the universality of Jesus Christ.

Dominus Iesus

Written in response to growing struggles with issues of pluralism, *Dominus Iesus*, the Declaration on the Unicity and Salvific Universality of Jesus Christ and the Church, published by the Congregation of the Doctrine of the Faith on August 6, 2000, intends to set the record straight on several theological issues, namely, the role of Jesus Christ as universal Savior, the necessity of the Church, universal salvation, and the Church's relations with non-Catholic Christians and members of other religious traditions. This document has inspired many critical responses from both within the Catholic community and in ecumenical circles about its treatment of universal salvation and the religions of the world because it presents views that contrast with the openness of the documents of the Second Vatican Council.

In his letter to bishops, Joseph Ratzinger (now Benedict XVI), the prefect who signed the declaration, presents these reasons for publishing the declaration:

> The Congregation for the Doctrine of the Faith has noted the growing presence of confused and erroneous ideas and opinions both within the Church generally and in certain theological circles regarding the doctrine of the unicity and universality of the salvific event of Jesus Christ, the unicity and unity of the Church...and the necessity of the Church for salvation...The declaration presents the principal truths of the Catholic faith in these areas; such truths require, therefore, irrevocable assent by the Catholic faithful; the text also refutes errors, clarifies some ambiguities and points out important questions that remain open to theological investigation and debate. Since it is a document of the Congregation for the Doctrine of the Faith, the declaration has a universal magisterial nature...Particularly in the areas of ecumenical and inter-religious dialogue and in Catholic universities and faculties of theology, it is essential that the doctrinal contents of this declaration become a point of reference as well as a solid and indispensable foundation for pastoral and missionary work which is convincing, effective and consistent with Catholic teaching.[101]

Hence, the declaration comes in response to the "errors" and "ambiguities" that have been put forward in areas of ecumenical and interreligious dialogue. The first half of the declaration is directed toward clergy and theologians who are in dialogue with the religions of the world. It cautions scholars against minimizing the role of Jesus Christ and separating the activity of the *Logos* and the Holy Spirit from the Savior. Jesus is the only Savior and his unique role must be upheld whenever one engages in dialogue with the religions of the world.

The declaration emphasizes that salvation is possible for all people, regardless of religious affiliation; however, following the lead of the Second Vatican Council, it points to Christ as the ultimate source of salvation. Jesus is the only Savior of the world, "who through the event of his incarnation, death and resurrection has brought the history of salvation to fulfillment."[102] It is contrary to the faith, the congregation declares, to deny the "unicity and salvific universality of the mystery of Jesus Christ."[103]

Salvation, then, is accomplished once and for all in Jesus Christ. While the congregation discusses how the "historical figures and positive elements" of other religions may fall within the "divine plan of salvation," it continues to uphold the unicity of Jesus Christ as the only Savior. Following the direction of the council, the congregation holds as contrary to the faith "solutions that propose a salvific action of God beyond the unique mediation of Christ."[104] Jesus has a role that is unique to him alone. In other words, he is the only and universal Savior for all of creation.

This boldness comes in response to scholars who deny or challenge the unicity of Christ and charge that his salvific role is universal but not absolute. Furthermore, while the declaration affirms the universal salvific will of God, it rejects the proposition that the Church is "one way of salvation alongside those constituted by other religions, seen as complementary to the church or substantially equivalent to her, even if these are said to be converging with the church toward the eschatological kingdom of God."[105] While the declaration repeats the affirmation made at the council that other religions contain "elements which come from God,"[106] it turns to *Redemptoris Missio* and the scriptures (1 Cor 10:20–21) when it holds that "rituals, insofar as they depend on superstitions, or other errors…, constitute an obstacle to salvation."[107] Further, the congregation speaks out against the dangers of religious relativism and, in a spirit of defense, bypasses the openness and tolerance of the Second Vatican Council:

> If it is true that the followers of other religions can receive divine grace, it is also certain that *objectively speaking*, they are in a gravely deficient situation in comparison with those who, in the church, have the fullness of the means of salvation.[108]

Hence, the Church must remain missionary so as to bring the fullness of truth to all people. "God wills the salvation of everyone through the knowledge of the truth, since salvation is found in truth."[109] Thus missionary activity is necessary as the Church wishes to deliver people from their "gravely deficient" situation. No doubt, this view received criticism from people throughout the world as scholars compare this view with the openness of the Second Vatican Council, as expressed in *Lumen Gentium*:

> Those who, through no fault of their own, do not know the Gospel of Christ or his Church, but who nevertheless seek God with a sincere heart, and moved by grace, try in their actions to do his will as they know it through the dictates of their conscience—these too may attain eternal salvation.[110]

While the congregation notes that "followers of other religions can receive divine grace," it does not view their religions as authentic paths to salvation. Thus, the salvific will of God is limited due to other religions' practices, prayers, and rituals. However, *Dominus Iesus* did take the opportunity to remind Catholic Christians that their salvation is also dependent upon their thoughts and actions: "Even though incorporated into the Church, one who does not persevere in charity is not saved…Or if they fail to respond (to the grace of Christ) in thought, word, and deed to that grace, not only shall they not be saved, but they shall be more severely judged" (LG 14). Does this not suggest that some Christians may find themselves in a "gravely deficient situation"?

Dominus Iesus was written in response to recent theological developments. Thus, its tone is much more defensive than that found in previous documents. More recently, during the pontificate of Benedict XVI, *Responses to Some Questions Regarding Certain Aspects of the Doctrine on the Church* (2007) was issued by the Congregation for the Doctrine of the Faith This document reaffirms that the Catholic Church is the one, true Church; however, the presence of "elements of truth and sanctification" in other Christian communities is acknowledged. While this short document does not address members of other religious traditions, it sets out to tackle some ecumenical concerns and to clarify the teaching of the Second Vatican Council: "the church of Christ subsists in the Catholic Church." The congregation asserts that "the word subsists can only be attributed to the Catholic Church" due to the "mark of unity" found in it and in the sacraments. However, the church of Christ is "present and operative in the churches and ecclesial communities not yet fully in communion with the Catholic Church"; therefore, the "Spirit of Christ has not refrained from using them as instruments of salvation." While the congregation affirms that *subsists in* "indicates the full identity of the church of Christ with the Catholic Church," theologians and other Christians may challenge this recent interpretation. Nevertheless, the document continues to teach that other Christian communities serve as "instruments of salvation." In the same year, the International Theological Commission published *The Hope for Salvation*, in which the destiny of infants who die without baptism is discussed. The document emphasizes the universal salvific will of God and hope of salvation for these infants:

> In the context of the discussion on the destiny of those infants
> who die without Baptism, the mystery of the universal salvific

> will of God is a fundamental and central principle. The depth
> of this mystery is reflected in the paradox of divine love which
> is manifested as both universal and preferential. (43)

The document goes on to affirm that "nobody is excluded from this salvific will" (46), not even infants who die without baptism. Here the theory of limbo is challenged and put to rest.

While Benedict XVI himself has issued no major document on the universal salvific will of God, it is helpful to end this chapter with his view on the parable of the last judgment. Recall how Fulgentius of Ruspe misused this parable to put forward his teaching on *extra ecclesiam nulla salus*: "pagans but also Jews or heretics and schismatics, cannot share in eternal life and will go into the everlasting fire which was prepared for the devil and his angels." The misuse of this parable went on to influence official Church teaching and led people to believe this parable referred to those outside the Church. In his first encyclical published in 2005, *Deus Caritas Est*, Benedict XVI refers to the proper interpretation of this parable and reminds Christians that love determines one's worth:

> Last, we should especially mention the great parable of the Last
> Judgment (cf. Mt. 25:31–46), in which love becomes the crite-
> rion for the definitive decision about a human life's worth or
> lack thereof. Jesus identifies himself with those in need, with
> the hungry, the thirsty, the stranger, the naked, the sick and
> those in prison. "As you did it to one of the least of these my
> brethren, you did it to me" (Mt. 25:40). Love of God and love
> of neighbor have become one: In the least of the brethren we
> find Jesus himself, and in Jesus we find God. (15)

Therefore, according to a proper reading of the parable, we are reminded that the righteous will be rewarded with "eternal life." Those who were condemned to "eternal punishment" were those who "did not" show love and compassion "to one of the least of these" (Matt 25:45) and did not refer to those who found themselves outside the Church.

3
Recent Contributions by Catholic Theologians

The mystery of God's plan to save all people continues to be a focus for many Catholic leaders and thinkers. Recall John Paul II's request for more theological reflection on this topic:

> There remain many questions which we have to develop and articulate more clearly. How does God work in the lives of people of different religions? How does his saving activity in Jesus Christ effectively extend to those who have not professed faith in him? In coming years, these questions and related ones will become more and more important for the Church in a pluralistic world, and pastors with the collaboration of experienced theologians, must direct their studious attention to them.[1]

While many insightful Catholic scholars have considered John Paul II's request,[2] this chapter looks at the contributions made by three prominent Catholic theologians: Jacques Dupuis, Paul F. Knitter, and Gavin D'Costa. Each in his own way has offered views that challenge, affirm, and contrast with official Church teaching. The first theologian to be considered, Jacques Dupuis, is one who presented insights that have challenged magisterial teaching. The discussion on Dupuis is longer than that on the others, as his work has been investigated by the Congregation for the Doctrine of the Faith. Any fair assessment merits a closer look at his work and the investigation it inspired.

Jacques Dupuis (1923–2004)

Jacques Dupuis, a Jesuit theologian and, before his death, professor at the Gregorian University, published his two most recent books and articles on this topic. Moreover, he took John Paul II's questions quite seriously. His contributions are important for several reasons. First, they move the discussion of theology of religions a step further than the position currently held by the official documents of the Catholic Church. Second, his work has inspired a response from the Congregation for the Doctrine of the Faith. The congregation issued on February 27, 2001, a notification concerning his 1997 publication *Toward a Christian Theology of Religious Pluralism*. That his work has been met with such a controversial response by the congregation merits his inclusion in this chapter on the current debate on the universal salvific will of God. Of interest, however, is the response that Dupuis and other theologians studying theology of religions have received. This chapter follows Dupuis's contributions and considers his "inclusive pluralism," his position on the universality of Jesus Christ, and his view of the salvific work of the Word and the Spirit in the world's religions.

In his article "Universality of the Word and Particularity of Jesus Christ," Dupuis begins his commentary with a brief summary of his book *Toward a Christian Theology of Religious Pluralism*. He notes that his book put forward a model for a theology of religious pluralism that would preserve "clearly the constitutive value of Jesus Christ for the salvation of humankind" and "would help recognize the salvific significance of the paths to salvation proposed by other religious traditions and their followers."[3] He names this model the "Trinitarian and Pneumatic Christology" model. This model, he

P. 112

suggests, could be used to solve the apparent dilemma between the two above affirmations. These solutions involve

> uniting three complementary and convergent ways in which, within the one divine plan for humankind, salvation reaches to persons in the concrete circumstances of their life. The three elements to be combined are: 1) the lasting actuality and universal efficacy of the event of Jesus Christ, notwith-standing the historical particularity of the event; 2) the universal operative presence of the Word of God whose action is not restricted by the human existence assumed by him in the mystery of the incarnation; 3) the equally universal action of the Spirit of God, which is neither limited nor exhausted by its outpouring through the risen and glorified Christ.[4]

Dupuis intends to show that while Jesus Christ is constitutive of salvation, other religions have a salvific role for their followers through the unbound work of the Word of God and the Spirit. The salvific activity of the Word and the Spirit, he suggests, accounts "for a plurality of paths designed by God for human salvation."[5] For Dupuis, God's desire to save all people is made clear through the work of the Word and the Spirit in other religions. This "inclusivist theology," he notes, "is compatible with a pluralistic model, insofar as there appears to be no contradiction in holding together the uniqueness of Jesus Christ as savior and a positive role in God's plan for other religious paths."[6] He calls this paradigm "inclusivist pluralism."[7] Within this paradigm "Christianity remains uniquely privileged":

> The Jesus Christ event represents the deepest and unsurpass-able self-commitment of God to humankind, to which all other personal involvements of God in human history are necessarily related and in which they find their hermeneutical key.[8]

While Christianity has a special place in God's salvific design, Dupuis cautions against assigning too great an importance to the salvific role of religions. He is interested in how God's desire to save people is worked out in all religions. First, he notes "God—and God alone—saves…In the Hebrew Bible, the title 'Savior' belongs principally to God; in the New Testament, it is applied only to God and to Jesus Christ…God saves through Jesus Christ (see Jn. 3:16–17)."[9] He charges that it is an abuse of language, then, to posit that religions save. Religions, rather, should be considered "channels" of God's salvation. Moreover, he finds it necessary to define the concept of salvation and combine it with the equally important and complementary concept of liberation that, contends Dupuis, is easily applicable to other religions:

> Without prejudice to the vast differences from one tradition to another, one may risk proposing a universal concept of salvation/liberation as follows: it has to do with the search for, and attainment of, fullness of life, wholeness, self-realization and integration. Whether, notwithstanding the many diverse concepts of salvation/liberation proposed by the various traditions, the reality of human salvation must, from a Christian theological viewpoint, be conceived after one common model for all human beings, is a question to which we must return in the light of recent discussion.[10]

This salvation/liberation is desired for all human beings (1 Tim 2:4). For Dupuis, God transmits this desire to save all people through "the inclusive presence in history of the mystery of Jesus Christ; the universal power of the Logos; and the unbound action of the Spirit."[11] Dupuis posits that God's saving action in Jesus Christ reaches members of other religions through a certain "mediation" of their own religious traditions.[12] Their own religions, then, play a role in the process of salvation/liberation. This is due, he contends, to the power of the *Logos* and the Spirit. Let us first consider his view on the universal action of the Word.

It is here that Dupuis intends to show the interrelatedness between the "universal operative presence of the Word of God and the unique saving significance of the historical event of Jesus Christ."[13] While he claims that there is no "contradiction or opposition" between the Word and Jesus Christ, he does not limit the power of the *Logos* to its "historically becoming human in Jesus Christ":

> But the Christ-event, however inclusively present, does not exhaust the power of the Word of God, who became flesh in Jesus Christ. The Prologue of the Gospel according to John makes explicit reference to Word's universal action throughout history: "The true light, which enlightens everyone, was coming into the world" (Jn. 1:9).[14]

Dupuis now brings us back to the *Logos*-theologies of the early fathers.[15] He recalls that it is the "illuminating power" of the *Logos*, present from the beginning, which accounts for the salvation of people before the time of the incarnation. Supporting his argument with the work of the fathers, he reminds his readers that people could be "enlightened" by the *Logos* who is the source of light, truth, and wisdom. Following the insights of Justin Martyr, Irenaeus, and Clement of Alexandria, Dupuis writes:

> Not only could the individual persons—Socrates, the Buddha, and so on— receive divine truth from the *Logos*; but human undertakings also—Greek philosophy and wisdom, as well as Asian wisdom—were the channels through which divine light reached to persons.[16]

Hence, Dupuis notes that one need only recall the work of the early fathers to conclude that the religions of the world contain elements of "truth and grace" (AG 9), given to them by the power of the *Logos*. Thus, Dupuis credits the *Logos* with the work of sowing seeds of truth and saving grace in the different religions. It is the same *Logos* that was once incarnate in Jesus Christ that is at work in the world today. While the Word of God is known in the person of Jesus Christ, the eternal *Logos* continues to communicate God's call to salvation to all people:

> It need not be denied that the eternal Logos could manifest itself to other peoples through other religious symbols...In continuity with a long Christian tradition of the Logos-theology that goes back as far as Justin Martyr...it may be held that the divine person who appears in Jesus is not exhausted by that historical appearance. The symbols and myths of other religions may point to the one who Christians recognize as the Christ.[17]

The Word, then, has been at work before and after the incarnation. That the action of the Word is not confined to its "historical appearance" in the person of Jesus Christ suggests for Dupuis that other religions can be considered as "conveyers of a divine action of the Word of God and as channels of divine salvation."[18] It is this insight that has been challenged by both the Congregation for the Doctrine of the Faith and other critics.

It is clear that Dupuis has moved the discussion on the theology of religions a step further. He has moved toward an "inclusivist pluralism" that allows other religions to function on their own and not serve as a mere preparation for the gospel. Regarding other religions as mere stepping stones is not enough for Dupuis. However, while Dupuis desires to move beyond the limits of past theologies of religion, he pulls himself back into speaking about a certain completion in Christianity. He wants to acknowledge other paths made available by God through the action of the Word and the Spirit, but he desires to maintain Christ's special place in God's salvific plan for humanity.

Dupuis sees his role of theologian as being more than that of an apologist. Rather, he seeks to develop and explain official Church teaching and be true to the vocation of theologian. For yesterday, today, and tomorrow the universal salvific will of God extends grace to all people in the hope that all people will respond and work toward establishing the reign of God. This salvific will is accomplished in Jesus Christ and continues through the action of the Word and the "unbound" Spirit. It is clear that all three persons on the Trinity act to save people; however, Dupuis continues to affirm the depth of God's self-communication in Jesus Christ. Dupuis works to develop certain insights as he seeks to understand God's salvific dealings with humanity. The early writers praised those who lived before the Christ-event for their commitment to wisdom, knowledge, and truth. God's desire to save all people began with creation and continues today. Dupuis acknowledges the ways in which members of other religions desire to do God's will as they pursue truth, goodness, and wisdom. For him, the universal salvific will of God is not limited by the visible or invisible boundaries of the Church nor is it restricted to the historical presence of God in the person of Jesus Christ. Dupuis is interested in how all people respond to God's action among them calling them to salvation/liberation. The action of God's Word and Spirit will bring this about. Luke's Gospel includes the parable of the sower in which Jesus affirms that the "seed" is the word of God (8:11). For those who hear and accept the word with "honest and good hearts" God will promise faith and salvation (8:12). These people will bear fruit due to their "patient endurance" (8:15). Similar to this parable, Dupuis is extending the universal salvific will of God to all people with "honest and good hearts" who follow God with "patient endurance."

Dupuis calls for a "universal theology of religions" that emphasizes the need for Christianity to dialogue with other religions. He acknowledges the plurality of beliefs around the world and attributes a positive value to them. What is key is that Dupuis is breaking new ground in his challenge to move Christians to reconsider ways in which salvation is mediated to members of other religions. He has embraced the enormous task of reexamining Christian teachings on the universal salvific will of God in light of the religious experience of billions of people around the world. It was his contribution and that of others that motivated the Congregation for the Doctrine of the Faith to respond with its notification on *Toward a Christian Theology of Religious Pluralism* and its declaration *Dominus Iesus*. Dupuis's thought has challenged many to rethink their views on the universal salvific will of God. Another Catholic theologian who has done so is Paul F. Knitter. Let us consider his views.

Paul F. Knitter

Paul F. Knitter is a Roman Catholic eco-liberation theologian and a pluralist. In his work he supports a global and interreligious theology. In more than forty years of scholarly work he has moved from Christocentricity to theocentricity to emphasizing global responsibility through socio-political-ecological concern. He would consider himself an interreligious dialoguer who has developed many interreligious friendships.

On the occasion of his retirement from Xavier University, he presented his reflections on his "call" to interreligious dialogue.[19] The "vocation of an interreligious theologian," he notes, "is really the meeting and, as it were, mating of two vocations, two calls that make very real and definite and often contrasting claims on the same person."[20]

He has attempted to follow one path that consists of two calls—to be "a Catholic theologian and to be an interreligious dialoguer." Early in his career, he felt drawn to dialogical praxis. He began teaching "dialogue with" courses and moved to clarify "the way, or method, of interreligious dialogue."[21] What he was encountering in other religious traditions, other religious books, and friendships was "necessary for salvation." His encounter with other religions, then, helped him to become a better Christian theologian: "To be a theologian in any one tradition—or, let me be more careful: to be a 'relatively adequate' theologian in any one tradition—one must be, at least to some extent, a theologian of another tradition."[22] These studies and experiences have influenced his thought on the universal salvific will of God.

For Knitter, God is greater than any one mediator, including Jesus, and he suggests that other religions are salvific when they promote the values of the kingdom of God. The universal salvific will of God is made known through different mediators, at different times, and in different religious traditions. He offers an approach that is both regnocentric and soteriocentric and he supports a "plurality of authentically true-and-salvific religious traditions."[23] Salvation, for him, is meant to improve the world:

> An interreligious, ethical dialogue is taking place, and gaining speed. It seems to suggest, if not prove, that within all the religions there is a concern to improve the lot of human beings in this world, which means improving this world. Whatever "salvation" or "enlightenment" or moksha may mean for the interior life of the soul or for life after death, it also is meant to make a difference in life on this earth.[24]

Hence, for Knitter, salvation is a gift God desires all people to experience in this world as well as in the next.

The mystery of God, suggests Knitter, "cannot be held by any one religion or revelation or savior...this mystery (of God) is not simply one but plural."[25] The God Knitter knows in Jesus and whose reign he works for is

> a God of pure, unbounded love, a God who seeks to communicate with all persons and who wills to inspire all men and women to work for a world of love and justice. This is a God who cannot be confined, a God who, in speaking truly in Jesus, reveals that God cannot speak only in Jesus.[26]

Knitter, then, puts forward the thesis that "the uniqueness of Jesus' salvific role can be reinterpreted."[27] For him, Jesus is truly a savior, not the only savior. *Truly*, for Knitter, means "decisively, universally, and indispensably."[28] Jesus, Knitter suggests, "is the way open to other ways" and "Christ is the way that can, and often must challenge other ways."[29]

While "the uniqueness of Jesus contains Christianity's essential and distinctive contribution to the interreligious dialogue,"[30] Knitter prefers to emphasize the two commandments of Jesus: love of God and love of neighbor. "In Jesus we Christians have felt with our hands and seen with our eyes God's preferential concern for the marginalized...There are many 'truth claims' that are essential to what God has revealed in Jesus; this is certainly one of them."[31] Salvation, then, involves loving others and working toward the betterment of our communities, locally and globally. All people, regardless of religious affiliation, need salvation and God is ready to answer the diverse needs of members of all religious traditions. Salvation, for Knitter, involves "a call and empowerment to transform this world from one of division and injustice into one of love and mutuality."[32] This human betterment includes an ecological element. All of God's creation is in need of salvation. The salvation God wills and preached by Jesus, Knitter contends, is universal and inclusive:

> if Christianity at one time defined its uniqueness in the dictum *extra ecclesiam nulla salus* (outside the church no salvation) today it finds that uniqueness in the proclamation *extra mundum nulla salus* (outside the world no salvation); that is, unless we are realizing salvation or well-being in and for this world, we are not realizing the salvation announced by Jesus. This is the unique ingredient in his saving message.[33]

Christianity, suggests Knitter, is a "universal religion" that must engage in missionary activity in order to "share its vision of truth and well being with others."[34] Salvation, then, has individual, communal, and global implications and can be accessed through one's own religious tradition and due to the mediation of diverse saviors. While, for Knitter, Jesus makes a unique contribution to the understanding of the meaning of salvation, God is working salvifically throughout the religions of the world and their various mediators. However, in his search for a dialogical Christology, he has come to "understand and follow Jesus as the way that both challenges other ways by its distinctiveness and at the same time is open to being challenged by what makes other ways distinct."[35]

Gavin D'Costa

Gavin D'Costa is a Roman Catholic theologian who has reconsidered the limits of inclusivism and pluralism. He was born of Indian parents in Kenya and received his doctorate in Cambridge, England. He began teaching in London and his doctorate work was on John Hick. He has advised the Pontifical Council for other Faiths and in 1993 he started teaching in Bristol, England. His multicultural background and experience have served to inspire his work as a theologian interested in interreligious dialogue.

From his first book, *Theology and Religious Pluralism* (1986), to *The Meeting of Religions and the Trinity* (2000), D'Costa has made significant contributions to the study of religions and the ongoing debate on Christianity and pluralism. In 1987, John Hick and Paul F. Knitter published a number of essays in a book entitled *The Myth of Christian Uniqueness*. In response, D'Costa published *Christian Uniqueness Reconsidered: The Myth of a Pluralistic Theology of Religions* (1990). D'Costa claims that Christianity is distinctive due to its trinitarian theology.

He affirms that Christianity is fully true and salvific. For him, God desires to save all people, but God respects our freedom. This means that we cannot be certain that we will be saved, "although we have no right to be pessimistic about the outcome." He challenges the various positions of pluralists and attempts to draw on the riches of his own Roman Catholic Christian tradition to understand how God is at work in other religious traditions. His approach to other religions is trinitarian: "Jesus is the normative criterion of God, while not foreclosing the on-going self-disclosure of God in history, through the Spirit."[36]

D'Costa is an inclusivist theologian who suggests that "an appropriate doctrine of the Trinity" can address many of the concerns put forward by pluralists. Through the persons of the Trinity, the universal salvific will of God is communicated beyond the confines of Christianity:

> There are no good theological reasons to suggest that God's activity has stopped, but rather, given the universal salvific will of the Father revealed in Christ, we can have every expectation that God's activity in history is ongoing and certainly not historically limited to Christianity. The logical point I am making is this: All history, both past and to come, is potentially a particularity by which God's self-revelation is mediated. Chronologically and geographically there cannot be present limitations to this: "The Spirit blows where it will." Ecclesiologically, this is affirmed in the condemnation of the Jansenist teaching that "outside the church no grace is granted"…The important point is that this acknowledgement of the saving activity of God outside the Church requires that non-Christians must have a narrative space within Christian theology and practice so that their histories and stories can be heard without distortion.[37]

D'Costa acknowledges the need for mutual fulfillment of religions[38] and he uses his trinitarian tradition to show how God relates to the world in different ways.

His most recent position is found in *The Meeting of Religions and the Trinity*. He challenges the pluralist position and suggests that a trinitarian approach to interreligious dialogue assists in understanding how God's salvific will works on other religious traditions. He roots his discussion in the ecclesial documents of the Second Vatican Council to the present day. He tries to show that "since Vatican II the Roman Catholic church advances a position on other religions that is highly Trinitarian and allows for the active sanctifying role of the Holy Spirit to be present within other religions that cannot be predicted by the church."[39] While the conciliar and postconciliar documents "do not legitimate pluralism or inclusivism," he builds on them and works to consider the "ecclesial significance" of other religions without compromising his trinitarian beliefs.

In the first half of the book D'Costa discusses the pluralism of John Hick and Paul F. Knitter. He continues his discussion with an assessment of the pluralist views of members of other religious traditions: Judaism (Dan Cohn-Sherbok), Hinduism (Sarvapelli Radhakrishan), and Buddhism (the Dalai Lama). D'Costa concludes that they are "pluralist" only in rhetoric. In the second half of the book he presents a Christian understanding of other religious traditions rooted in a Roman Catholic trinitarian theology. Throughout his works he affirms that the salvific will of God is disclosed by the Spirit and illuminated by Christ. The universal saving action of the Spirit is linked to the incarnate Word.

D'Costa suggests that Christians should view other religious traditions from the perspective of the Holy Spirit; the Spirit is active in other religious traditions. This belief, he contends, should lead Christians to accept the universality of God's offer of salvation: "The Church stands under the judgment of the Holy Spirit, and if the Holy Spirit is active in the world religions, then the world religions are vital to Christian faithfulness."[40]

The universal salvific will of God, observes D'Costa, is made known through each of the persons of the Trinity. It is time, he suggests, to discover and acknowledge the salvific activity of the Holy Spirit and how it is part of God's universal salvific will.

D'Costa addresses the tension between the different positions put forward in theological discussion. On the one hand, the Holy Spirit is present in other religious traditions; on the other hand, there is some confusion as to whether these traditions mediate salvation. The universal action of the Spirit makes salvation available to all people. However, D'Costa is cautious about using "abstract talk of the 'presence of the Spirit' in other religions."[41] While D'Costa affirms the universal salvific will of God, he is careful to connect the salvific work of the Holy Spirit to Christ and the Church.

4
Recent Contributions by
Other Christian Theologians

While it is not within the scope of this book to offer a comprehensive study of the contributions made by other Christian theologians, or even the ones considered here, I discuss three influential Protestant scholars who have inspired the work of other theologians from diverse traditions. The final chapter includes a brief look at some contributions made by Orthodox scholars to the discussion of the salvific activity of the Holy Spirit. Catholic, Protestant, and Orthodox theologians have inspired each other in their study of the universal salvific will of God, each offering a unique approach to the topic.

John Hick

John Hick is an influential pluralist. In 1973, he called for a Copernican revolution in the theology of religions. He posited that God should be at the center of all thinking, not Christianity. In his writings he has challenged the teaching that Christ and the church are the only means to salvation. His experience and study of other religions have moved him to acknowledge and affirm the truth, goodness, and holiness found in other religious traditions.

His shift to theocentrism challenged the traditional teaching on the divinity of Christ and in his latest writings he has moved away from theocentrism and has embraced "Reality-centeredness." He argues that all religions are salvific insofar as they lead to the one divine Real. His use of the term *Real* or *Reality* attempts to capture the personal and impersonal natures of the divine present in other religious traditions.

Currently Hick is a fellow at the Institute for Advanced Research in the Humanities at Birmingham University in the United Kingdom. Also, he is professor emeritus at Claremont Graduate School. He was baptized as a baby in the Church of England and pursued the Christian life as a fundamentalist. Later on he ministered in the Presbyterian Church of England.

In his work he challenges the so-called superiority of Christianity and suggests that if Christianity was morally superior to other religious traditions would not the fruits of the Holy Spirit be more evident among Christians? He contends that pluralism is true because there is no moral advantage to being a Christian. Furthermore, a merciful, compassionate God who desires to save all people, even in their own traditions, is the focus of his work: "And could it really be an expression of infinite love to send the majority of the human race to eternal torment in hell?"[1] In response to this dilemma he draws on his experience and study of other religious traditions. He has called for a reinterpretation of what it means to be saved in all religious traditions.

In an earlier work, Hick established that the New Testament describes salvation as a "way" and concludes that salvation has more to do with right behavior than it does with right doctrine.[2] He calls for a more universal reflection on salvation:

> If we define salvation as being forgiven and accepted by God because of Jesus' death on the cross, then it becomes a tautology that Christianity alone knows and is able to preach the source of salvation. But if we define salvation as an actual human change, a gradual transformation from natural

self-centeredness (with all the human evils that flow from
this) to a radically new orientation centered on God and
manifested in the "fruit of the Spirit," then it seems clear
that salvation is taking place within all the world religions—
and taking place, so far as we can tell, to more or less the
same extent. On this view, which is not based on theological
theory, but on the observable realities of human life, salvation is not a juridical transaction inscribed in heaven, nor is
it a future hope beyond this life (although it is this too), but
it is a spiritual, moral, and political change that can begin
now and whose present possibility is grounded in the structure of reality.[3]

Following this logic, Hick suggests that other religions are
salvific. Salvation moves one away from natural self-centeredness
to Reality-centeredness. This transformation should bring peace,
joy, and compassion for others. It is in this way that one can determine whether a religion is salvific. While *salvation* is a term most
known to Christians, he takes into consideration the salvific elements of other religious traditions and thus, like Jacques Dupuis,
he prefers to use the hybrid term *salvation/liberation*:

And what is variously called salvation or liberation or
enlightenment or awakening consists in this transformation
from self-centredness to Reality- centredness. For brevity's
sake, I'll use the hybrid term "salvation/liberation." I suggest that this is the central concern of all the great world religions. They are not primarily philosophies or theologies but
primarily ways of salvation/liberation.[4]

Hick concludes that "not only Christianity, but also these
other world faiths, are human responses to the ultimate."[5] He
affirms the limitless, universal salvific will of God present in all
religious traditions:

Is it compatible with the limitless divine love that God
should have decreed that only a minority of human beings,

those who have happened to be born in a Christian part of the world, should have the opportunity of eternal life?[6]

He goes on to critique the position of exclusivists:

> Their position (exclusivists) is a consistent and coherent one for those who can believe that God condemns the majority of the human race, who have never encountered or who have not accepted the Christian gospel, to external damnation. Personally, I would view such a God as the Devil. But, more fundamentally, if we mean by salvation an actual salvific change in women and men, then it is an observable fact that this is not restricted either to any section of Christianity or Christianity as a whole.[7]

In several of his works, he reminds his readers that "in the great majority of cases…, the religion in which a person believes and to which he adheres depends upon where he was born."[8] Hence, God's saving activity cannot be limited to any one tradition. Any limitation, for Hick, would suggest that God's universal salvific will is limited. He views the different major religions as more or less equal paths to God, or the Real. Christianity, then, is not the one, true way to God, but one of many. Hick has summed up this view by quoting a passage from the *Bhagavad Gita:* "Howsoever men may approach me, even so I accept them; for, on all sides, whatever path they choose is mine." God's desire to save, then, is not exclusivistic:

> Can we then accept the conclusion that the God of love who seeks to save all mankind had nevertheless ordained that men must be saved in such a way that only a small minority can in fact receive this salvation?[9]

Hick, then, is opposed to any thought of hell or eternal damnation.[10] He prefers the optimism of the concept of universal salvation. While he considers the more exclusivistic scriptures, he contends that other scriptures do not rule out universalism.[11] He rejects any thought of permanent damnation and prefers to speak of gradations of condemnation. The universal salvific will of God, then, must extend beyond death. For Hick, salvation is a process, is contextual, and is offered to all people, living and dead.[12]

Salvific transformation, suggests Hick, has taken place when a person expresses "an inner peace, and joy and…compassionate love for others."[13] This salvific transformation is willed by God, the Real, in all religious traditions.

Clark Pinnock

Clark Pinnock is a Baptist theologian with inclusivist views. Pinnock retired from Baptist-related McMaster Divinity College in Hamilton, Ontario, Canada, where he was professor of Christian interpretation since 1977. He enters the discussion on the universal salvific will of God during controversial times: "The debate within the evangelical academy regarding salvation is intense and fierce, dominating all other discussions."[14] Several evangelical scholars agree[15] that "the classical evangelical position is under severe attack":

> in the mid 1980's, Clark Pinnock rejected traditional particularism, insisting that God's grace is sufficiently available in every culture to lead the unevangelized to salvation.[16]

In a paper entitled "Religious Pluralism: A Turn to the Holy Spirit," Pinnock addresses the current discussion on salvation outside the boundaries of Christianity: "How, therefore (people ask), could a just and merciful God consign to hell those whose very providential circumstances prevented them from hearing? Not only is this a painful dilemma intellectually but there exists some considerable hope among our people for a better resolution of this problem." In response to this question, Pinnock believes that God works "graciously" outside the limits of Christianity, calling all people to salvation. His views are inclusive, as he has hope in a merciful God whose desire to save is universal.

His inclusivist position on the universal salvific will of God has four key elements. First, he establishes that God loves people and has created us with the desire to enter in a relationship with God. Second, God seeks human collaboration in God's dealings with creation. Third, God exercises a general oversight over creation. Finally, God has given us free will and sanctifies us with our cooperation.[17]

> God in deciding to create humankind, placed higher value on freedom leading to love than on guaranteed conformity to his will.[18]

God, for Pinnock, is personal, temporal, omniscient, and resourceful and we are free to cooperate with God's will and be saved.

Pinnock abandoned some traditional evangelical views on the universal salvific will of God and insisted that God's grace is available and present in all religious traditions. Hence, God's grace could lead the unevangelized to salvation. He suggests that Christian theology must affirm universality and inclusion:

> Western theology has been reluctant to acknowledge that grace operates outside the church, and there is the abhorrent notion of a secret election to salvation of a specific number of sinners, not of people at large. Such beliefs are deep in the Western tradition and place the genuineness of God's universal salvific will in considerable doubt. My sense is that Christians today are less willing than before to accept such a hard and pessimistic theology.[19]

Hence, Pinnock strives to relate God's salvific will to the religious pluralism that exists. More and more he calls on Christians to consider God's boundless mercy as a truth that cannot be ignored.[20] However, elsewhere, he is clear to suggest that "we cannot say (just to be charitable) that all religions mediate God's grace and truth…We cannot assume from the fact of God's love for the world that every person on earth has been supplied with a true religion."[21] So while God's grace is present in other religious traditions, not everything in those traditions is true or salvific.

Inclusivism, he suggests, addresses the mystery of the universal salvific will of God. First, he notes that inclusivism engenders hope. Second, inclusivism affirms God's mercy and love for all people and extends God's grace to people of all religious traditions. Third, "inclusivism appeals because of its honest willingness to acknowledge sanctity in persons and religions other than Christian."[22] Fourth, this position affirms a "more coherent version of orthodoxy." This position features the limitless nature of the universal salvific will of God more than the exclusivist position. The universal presence of divine grace is best represented in the inclusivist position. All people are loved by God and God desires to bring salvation to them through the gift of God's grace.

Another attractive feature of Pinnock's theology is his emphasis on the salvific role of the Holy Spirit in other religious traditions. Here he acknowledges the influence of John Paul II:

> The Holy Spirit plays a prominent role in my understanding of inclusivism. I rejoice in John Paul II's decision to speak in these terms also…The Spirit is central to this model—not general revelation or the religions themselves, but the ubiquitous inspiration of the Spirit. Through the Spirit, God offers every person the mystery of his grace, because in their hearts, as the Council says, he works in unseen ways.[23]

Hence, similar to the teaching of the Second Vatican Council and John Paul II, Pinnock acknowledges the salvific activity of the Holy Spirit in other religious traditions. Through the universal work of the Holy Spirit God offers the gift of salvific grace. Pinnock pushes the universal nature of God's saving grace: "Are we not all burdened by the apparent unfairness of a message that we say has universal saving significance, but which has not actually been available to a sizable percentage of the race hitherto?"[24]

Again, inspired by the Second Vatican Council, Pinnock suggests that God's offer of grace assists one with one's honest search for God and one's use of conscience. Religions, then, may play a positive role in preparing one to receive the salvation of Jesus Christ. While billions of people may not know Jesus Christ, they may come to God through their own religious traditions and through their response to God's grace. "Everyone must eventually pass through Jesus to reach the Father, but there is more than one path for arriving at this place."[25] One may not come to know Jesus Christ in this lifetime, but one will know him in the afterlife. These religions are ways to Jesus Christ. The universal salvific will of God is extended to all people, whether they know it or not. However, for Pinnock, one issue remains:

> what about those who, when presented with the gospel, still choose to remain within their own faith—a Muslim, for example, who is drawn to Jesus but cannot break with his people? Perhaps he is afraid. My instinct is to leave this matter with the grace of God, who knows the factors that go into such a decision and makes valid judgments. Living in a country where there is no danger in becoming Christian, I am in no position to judge such a case. At the same time, it is no small matter to turn away from the grace of God (Heb. 2:1–3).[26]

Here Pinnock presents the challenge of presenting the gospel of Jesus Christ. One may be presented with the gospel, but may not accept it as truth because one may be comfortable and happy with one's own religious tradition. Or one may be fearful to convert. While the Second Vatican Council emphasized the importance of religious freedom and following one's conscience, Pinnock challenges other Christians to consider this issue.

Pinnock urges Christians to give serious attention to the church's teaching on the universal salvific will of God. In his works addressing this topic he challenges Christians to address issues related to superiority and chauvinism. However, as a devout Christian, he hopes that other Christians enter dialogue without compromising key beliefs and truth claims, for example, the incarnation.

S. Mark Heim

S. Mark Heim is an evangelical Christian theologian who has spent time in South Asia and has developed an openness to members of other religious traditions. In two major works he sets out to challenge the notion of one salvation awaiting all people. In his critique of recent efforts to understand universal salvation, Heim suggests that most parties to the discussion of universal salvation have assumed erroneously that one religious fulfillment awaits practitioners of all paths.

In *Salvations: Truth and Difference in Religion* Heim explores the idea of a diversity of salvations offered by different religious traditions. He argues that members of one tradition can recognize legitimate and genuine values in the very different ideals of another path while continuing to regard their own tradition as "normative and definitive." Hence, in this book, he refers to salvation in the plural, "salvations," because salvation in the singular has been so problematic. He suggests that the singular use of the term easily leads to exclusivism. Metaphysically, Heim posits that there is no reason why diverse religious fulfillments could not continue into the next world as well.

Heim begins his study with critiques of the major representatives of the pluralist camp, namely, John Hick, Wilfred Cantwell Smith, and Paul F. Knitter. While Heim appreciates the contributions made by each of these writers, he continues to critique their approaches to the universal salvific will of God and universal salvation. He charges that pluralist thought itself can smack of exclusivism when pluralists make their Western approaches normative for the rest of humanity.

Hence, pluralists, for Heim, may become what they want to avoid the most: the extreme of exclusivity. Heim attempts to avoid such tendencies. Instead, he proposes a new position that would allow for diversity among and uniqueness within traditions. Further, he maintains both the finality of Christ and the validity of other religious paths. He names this option "inclusivistic pluralism" or "orientational pluralism," a term he borrowed from philosopher Nicholas Rescher. Orientational pluralism, observes Heim, offers a more pluralistic hypothesis than other pluralist views: "there can be a variety of actual but different religious fulfillments,"[27] hence the term *salvations*.

In brief, orientational pluralism suggests that there are multiple religious ends or salvations. It represents one approach to pluralism. Heim recognizes the possible value of other religious traditions without trying to place them into one grand theory. However, herein lies the challenge of Heim's claim. Being an orthodox Christian, Heim posits that while Christians can and should make a judgment, they must add that such alternate non-Christian ends are "subordinate to the Christian end finally to be encompassed by it." Salvation through Christ is the most perfect fulfillment:

> The fundamental challenge of my proposal for Christians is to reflect on the possibility of the providential provision of a diversity of religious ends for human beings…On the other hand, the alternativeness of these ends to Christian aims allows and even requires a judgment from the Christian perspective that subordinates them to the consummation of the Christian life. To realize something other than communion with the triune God and with others in the continuing relationship of creating being is to achieve a lesser good.[28]

Consequently, Heim finds it necessary to rank religious fulfillments. He has struggled with the mystery of universal salvation while remaining faithful to his understanding of the Christian faith. Elsewhere, he turns to the work of the Holy Spirit to explain the providence of God's salvific will in other religious traditions:

> theological reflection turns to the work of the Spirit and focuses on the continued freedom and providence of God's action. The Spirit blows where it wills, and the religions can be viewed through the lens of the possibility of this direct, spontaneous action and presence of God: a possibility which is fulfilled whenever God's creation fulfills some portion of its ordained beauty, justice, and love.[29]

Similar to Dupuis, D'Costa, and John Paul II, Heim has turned to the salvific activity of the Spirit to explain God's salvific will for people of all religious traditions.

After writing *Salvations*, Heim went on to reconsider his understanding of the multiplicity of religious ends in *The Depth of the Riches: A Trinitarian Theology of Religious Ends*. In this book Heim develops his theology with a renewed focus on the belief of God as trinitarian and continues to speak of "penultimate religious fulfillments."

While Heim continues to be a "convinced inclusivist," he addresses the challenges of pluralism with a study of the doctrine of the Trinity. In *The Depth of the Riches* he defines salvation for Christians as "communion with God and God's creatures through Christ Jesus."[30] While Christians can experience the fullness of salvation rooted in the Trinity, members of other religions can experience limited "different, real religious ends that not Christian salvation at all."[31] Hence, different religious traditions offer their members different "religious ends." However, these religious ends are, for Heim, inferior, as Christian salvation is the ultimate end. These other religions can only offer "penultimate ends." God has given all people the freedom to choose their own path:

> God's saving will offers all the opportunity for communion in the triune life through Christ. But that same saving will

also brings to perfection each true relation with God that a person may freely choose as a final end. And beyond this, God brings the ensemble of such ends and choices to its own pluralistic perfection, integrating the chosen relations and goods so as to create the richest satisfaction of each and all under the terms of their desired fufillments.[32]

While this proposition affirms the mercy and providence of God, some critics of Heim's position[33] note that it may be unrealistic since many people inherit their religious traditions at birth—a fact addressed by John Hick. Millions of people may never be exposed to Christianity long enough to conclude that only Christianity offers the ultimate religious end.

In his most recent publication *Saved from Sacrifice: A Theology of the Cross*, Heim explores the significance and saving power of the cross. Drawing on the work of French biblical scholar Rene Girard, he develops a theology of atonement. Girard, notes Heim, "contends that the practice of sacrificial scapegoating is a cornerstone of human society and religion. Communities solve their internal conflicts by uniting against a chosen victim."[34] In the preface, he states that this recent work is a "book on Christology and salvation," where he explores the "saving act of God in the cross" and the "sinful human act." In affirming that Christ died for us, he goes on to say that "Christ took our place,"[35] "a sacrifice to end sacrifice."[36] In the cross, God vindicates the "victim of scapegoating sacrifice":

> What I have tried to say in this book is that there is a concrete rescue in the cross. There is the rescue and vindication of a victim of scapegoating sacrifice, and more broadly, there is a rescue of all of us from the thoughtless bondage to that violent way of maintaining peace and unity. This is a saving transaction, in which God is willing to be subjected to our persecution in order to deprive it of future victims and end its power. That is the simple rescue, on which the other meanings of the cross are built.[37]

Although the focus of the book is a theology of atonement, in presenting the saving significance of the cross for victims of scapegoating, Heim reaffirms the cultural and spiritual implications of Jesus' death for all humankind. Hence, the saving significance of the cross is universal.

5
Conclusions

While it was not within the scope of this work to offer a detailed analysis of all approaches to the universal salvific will of God, several insights emerged throughout our discussion. First, interreligious theologians are increasingly moving away from exclusivistic views and toward inclusivistic and pluralist views on the universal salvific will of God. Second, theologians are examining the salvific activity of the Holy Spirit. Third, they are attempting to define salvation for members of other religious traditions.

From Exclusive to Inclusive

The first five centuries saw a growing emphasis on Church membership and a valid baptism. While early writers such as Ignatius of Antioch, Ambrose of Milan, Origen, and Augustine addressed the connection between salvation and baptism, the First Council of Constantinople officially taught the need of embracing orthodoxy and baptism. Unfortunately, however, the struggle between competing churches gave birth to the axiom *extra ecclesiam nulla salus*. Cyprian, Augustine, and Fulgentius of Ruspe made use of the axiom as they insisted that those who refused to enter the Church were guilty of willful separation and rejection of the Church. Their views went on to influence the first step in official teaching of the Church on the universal salvific will of God and members of other religions.

The sixth through to the ninth centuries continued along this line as the official documents of the Church declared the necessity of the Church for salvation and the necessity of explicit faith in Jesus Christ. The Fourth Lateran Council in 1215 was the first ecumenical council to use the axiom *extra ecclesiam nulla salus*. Hence, it was officially taught that there was no hope for salvation outside the Church. In 1302, Boniface VIII not only declared no salvation outside the Church, but he insisted that one submit to the Roman pontiff in order to be saved. The Council of Florence (1431–45) was the first ecumenical council to add Jews and pagans to the list of the damned. Borrowing from Fulgentius of Ruspe's *Treatise on Faith*, Eugene IV (1431–47) taught that "all those who are outside the Catholic Church, not only pagans but also Jews or heretics and schismatics, cannot share in eternal life and will go into the everlasting fire which was prepared for the devil and his angels." While other thinkers, such as Dominicans and Jesuits, developed more inclusive ways of approaching the fate of those outside the Church, official teaching was consistent in its view that there was no salvation outside the Church.

The discovery of the New World, however, brought some new challenges and it is here that the Church develops new teachings to account for God's mercy and desire to save all people, even those outside the Church. The Council of Trent in 1547 officially taught baptism of desire, the second step in official teaching. Hence, for those who had never heard of Jesus Christ, faith in God represented a baptism of desire. Sometime later, in their response to Jansenism, Alexander VIII in 1690 and Clement XI in 1713 held that pagans, Jews, and others "do receive the motions of grace by which they can be saved." Pius IX and Pius XII moved the discussion of inculpable ignorance forward in the late nineteenth and twentieth centuries. Each of these teachings was founded upon the insights gained at the discovery of the New World and the reality that billions of people had not heard or accepted the gospel. God could not condemn those who, through no fault of their own, have not heard the gospel proclaimed. Pius IX emphasized the mercy of God toward the invincibly ignorant, and Pius XII taught that those who find themselves outside the Church can be ordained to the mystical body of Christ through an "unconscious desire and longing." The possibility of salvation for the inculpably ignorant represents the third step in official teaching. The shift toward inclusivity is most evident, however, in the teaching of the Second Vatican Council.

The Second Vatican Council, inspired by the insights of thinkers developing new ideas prior to the council, went on to declare officially that God desires the salvation of all people and it affirmed the presence of God's grace in other religions. Members of other religions could be saved by God's grace through Jesus Christ. Thus, those who try to do God's will, "as they know it through the dictates of their conscience," may attain salvation. Moreover, the Holy Spirit offers all the possibility to be saved and share in the paschal mystery. The teaching of the Second Vatican Council represents the fourth step in the move toward inclusivity. However, it is the move toward the fifth step, how the Spirit works in other religions, that has created the most fruitful dialogue to date.

A Deepened Pneumatology

The shift toward an inclusive understanding of salvation has shed light on a number of important issues. First, it was of interest to note how John Paul II wrote of an "integral salvation, one which embraces the whole person."[1] Thus, it was important to understand how salvation involves the whole person and not just the soul in the afterlife. Several of the theologians addressed in this work have discussed the salvation of the person in the present. This insight is important as it implies that salvation has present-day implications for all people. Furthermore, an inclusive understanding of salvation inspired theologies of the Holy Spirit.

The pneumatology of the Second Vatican Council inspired a decisive turn in the discussion of world religions and the universal salvific will of God. Accordingly, the magisterium had addressed and continued to develop the salvific activity of the Holy Spirit. Hence, similar to other theologians, the official documents have presented a trinitarian understanding of how salvation is achieved in persons of all faiths. *Gaudium et Spes* offered a sneak preview of the theology of the Holy Spirit that would develop after the council: "All this holds true not for Christians but for men of good will in whose hearts grace is active visibly. For since Christ died for all, and since all men are in fact called to one and the same destiny, which is divine, we must hold that the Holy Spirit offers to all the possibility of being made partners, in a way known to God, in the paschal mystery."[2] This text suggests something about the salvific activity of the Holy Spirit; after all, "the Holy Spirit was at work in the world before Christ was glorified."[3] John Paul II continued to move in this direction in *Dominum et Vivificantem* and *Redemptoris Missio.* It is the theology of John Paul II, then, that moves the Church's approach, and the approach of Dupuis, D'Costa, and Pinnock, on the universal salvific will of God to focus on the salvific role of the Spirit.

While John Paul II declares that salvation is always in Jesus Christ,[4] he affirms the "effect of the Spirit of truth operating outside the visible confines of the mystical body";[5] that the Spirit "blows where it wills";[6] that it is present in all authentic prayer;[7] that "the Holy Spirit in a manner known only to God offers to every man the possibility of being associated with the paschal mystery";[8] and that the grace of Christ is communicated through the Holy Spirit, enabling "each person to attain salvation through his or her free cooperation."[9] *Dialogue and Proclamation* develops these insights and continues to affirm the salvific role of the Holy Spirit.

In this document Jesus Christ remains the source of salvation, but "the mystery of salvation reaches out to them (members of other religions) in a way known to God through the invisible action of the Spirit of Christ."[10] Similarly, the International Theological Commission's document *Christianity and the World Religions* declared that all prayer is inspired by the Holy Spirit.[11] Moreover, it affirmed that God's salvific action works through all religions through the universal action of the Holy Spirit.[12] Also, the Spirit gives all the possibility of being saved and the "salvific value of religions as such must be situated in the context of the universal active presence of the Spirit of Christ."[13] Even *Dominus Iesus*, the most controversial of these documents, affirms the salvific role of the Holy Spirit. While it opposes the idea of the "unbound activity" of the Holy Spirit,[14] it declares that Jesus works in "communion with his Spirit"[15] to save people "beyond the visible boundaries of the church."[16] It goes on to quote *Gaudium et Spes* (22), which speaks of the Holy Spirit offering all people the possibility of sharing in the paschal mystery. However, all that the Spirit accomplishes in the other religions is to be understood "in reference to Christ, the Word who took flesh by the power of the Spirit."[17] *Dominus Iesus*, then, offers a trinitarian understanding of the universal salvific will of God:

> There is only one salvific economy of the one and triune God, realized in the mystery of the incarnation, death and resurrection of the Son of God, actualized with the cooperation of the Holy Spirit and extended in its salvific value to all humanity and to the entire universe.[18]

Thus, it is clear that the salvific work of the Spirit is noted in several key documents.

The official documents of the Church gradually begin to declare that salvation is possible outside the visible boundaries of the Church by the grace of God through Jesus Christ; then, the Holy Spirit works in other religions to bring salvation to their members. The move toward inclusivity, then, was accompanied by an emphasis on the salvific action of the three persons of the Trinity. Just as the Church set out to articulate how members of other religions are saved, it developed a trinitarian theology to account for it. Hence, as the Church moved away from the exclusivity of *extra ecclesiam nulla salus*, it moved toward new ways of explaining how the Trinity works to bring about salvation throughout the world. The action of the Spirit, then, has received growing attention from the magisterium and theologians. Paul F. Knitter writes:

> Viewing others from the perspective of the Spirit, Christians know that the reality of the Divine cannot be contained only in the activity of the Creator-Parent or of the Savior-Word, but that the Divine is also Spirit infusing other religions.[19]

The belief that God's Spirit is at work in other religions affirms God's universal action in the religions of the world. Similarly, Gavin D'Costa asserts that the Church must be open to acknowledging the presence and work of the Spirit in other religions:

> The Church stands under the judgment of the Holy Spirit, and if the Holy Spirit is active in the world religions, then the world religions are vital to Christian faithfulness...Without listening to this testimony Christians cease to be faithful to their own calling as Christians, in being attentive to God.[20]

However, D'Costa is careful to connect the action of the Spirit to the universality and particularity of Jesus Christ. For him, Jesus remains the norm by which to judge what the Spirit is disclosing:

> The riches of the mystery of God are disclosed by the Spirit and are measured and discerned by their conformity to and in their illumination of Christ...Jesus is the normative criterion of God, while not foreclosing the ongoing self-disclosure of God in history, through the Spirit.[21]

Hence, Jesus' salvific role must not be cast in the shadow of the work of the Spirit. Similarly, Walter Kasper suggests that "we must consider the question of the unity and unicity of Jesus Christ in the diversity of religions more closely from a Trinitarian and Christological confession. This will lead us to a kenotic analysis of the problem of unity and diversity."[22] God, Kasper writes,

> is self giving love in which the Father communicates with the Son and the Father; and the Son with the Holy Spirit. Each of the three persons is fully God, totally eternal, and each gives the others room in which they can communicate themselves and renounce themselves. In this kenotic way God is unity in diversity.[23]

Thus, the persons of the Trinity work in unity while allowing space for unique self-communication.

While Kasper and theologians such as Jacques Dupuis have pushed for a trinitarian understanding of the universal salvific will of God, others have appealed to a more developed understanding of pneumatology to feature the place of the Spirit. Furthermore, some theologians have revisited the implications of the *filioque* in order to understand better the role of the Spirit.

Amos Yong, a Pentecostal theologian, contends that the traditional Latin doctrine of the *filioque* does not allow for an adequate theology of the Holy Spirit.[24] In other words, Yong posits that Latin theology has subordinated the action of the Spirit to that of the Son. He calls for a shift in the theology of the religions whereby Christians are called to be more open to the presence of the Holy Spirit throughout the whole of creation.[25] Too much of an emphasis on Christology, he observes, presents roadblocks to sincere dialogue. A greater awareness of the universal activity of the Spirit can serve to lift such roadblocks.[26] It may be of interest to turn to Orthodox theology for insights.

Georg Khodr offers an Orthodox theology of the Holy Spirit that addresses the issue of religious pluralism.[27] Yong suggests that Khodr, like other Orthodox theologians,[28] is "convinced that the dominance of ecclesiology in Latin theology and its ecclesiologically defined soteriology was to be traced to the *filioque*."[29] This implies that the ecclesiology of the Latin West has inspired the *extra ecclesiam nulla salus* proposition. The Orthodox East, however, has emphasized "the concept of *oikinomia*."[30] Yong continues to explain the implications of the *filioque*:

> Briefly stated, the import of this perennial doctrinal problem restated in this context is this: If the Spirit is from the Father and or through the Son (as affirmed by the West in its addition of the *Filioque* to the Creed), it makes sense to think of the domain of the Spirit more as circumscribed by the domain of the Son and his body, the church, than not. If, however, on the proposed alternative reading, which is being increasingly accepted by a wide spectrum of theologians, the Spirit is from the Father of the Son, then the economy of the Son in no way limits that of the Spirit.[31]

The Orthodox understanding of the role of the Spirit suggests that the Spirit is not limited by the Son and his body, the church. This understanding suggests that the Spirit can act independently from the Son and his church. The official teaching of the Catholic Church has, since Vatican II, addressed the unique salvific activity of the Spirit in the official documents of the Church. The development of a pneumatological theology of religions, however, has not come without its share of inconsistencies and ambiguities.[32]

While *Dominus Iesus* affirms that there is one salvific economy working through Christ and the Spirit,[33] other documents speak of both the "Spirit of Christ"[34] and "the universal action of the Holy Spirit,"[35] and still others declare the unique work of the Spirit.[36] As Catholic theologies of the Holy Spirit continue to develop, they may be inspired by the work of Orthodox theologians as they seek to explain the unique action of the Spirit.[37]

A pneumatological theology of religions will continue to enhance the discussion of the universal salvific will of God. It will be interesting to see how future official documents and theologians will address the salvific action of the Spirit, given the discussion that has occurred. The magisterium is challenged to present a consistent and clear understanding of the role of the Spirit in the religions of the world. The study of the Holy Spirit will move theologians and the magisterium to consider ways in which salvation is communicated within religious traditions.

A Deepened Understanding of Salvation

A deepened theology of salvation will also improve interreligious dialogue.

It has been established that salvation is communicated within a community through the work of the Holy Spirit. However, this salvation is not limited to Christian communities; therefore, members of other religious traditions can be saved. This implies that their communities are significant for communicating salvation. Does this mean that these communities are "ways of salvation"?

In his book, *Crossing the Threshold of Hope*, John Paul II notes: "Here before all else, we need to explain the Christian doctrine of salvation and of the mediation of salvation, which always originates in God."[38] We know that God desires to give salvation to us;[39] we believe that we receive salvation in Jesus Christ;[40] we know that it is not limited to Christians;[41] we know that the Spirit is at work in the world, making salvation possible for all people;[42] yet, do we know what salvation is? Before we can speak of salvation and the other religious traditions, we need to understand what it is that we want others to experience. The official documents have been consumed with questions such as: Who is saved? How is one saved? Who saves us? Are members of other religious traditions saved? If yes, how are they saved? But Christians must also have a developed theology of salvation that could be presented to a member of another religious tradition. What is this salvation and from what do I need to be saved? If salvation is more than life after death (for example, Matt 8:23–27), then human beings need to be saved from more than simply punishment in the afterlife. Moreover, how does this salvation apply to members of other religious traditions and why do they need it too?

A fuller understanding of salvation, similar to that of Hick and Dupuis, would be beneficial for interreligious dialogue, since the experience of salvation is not desired by Christians alone. While many theologians have addressed the mystery of salvation,[43] different traditions may understand the meaning of salvation differently. The Orthodox tradition, for example, defines salvation as "union with God."[44] This definition connects to the Christian mystical tradition that sees union with God as the ultimate spiritual fulfillment.

A fuller theology of salvation would contribute to the larger "dialogue of salvation."[45] While no one definition of salvation can capture the mystery that surrounds God and the gift God gives, scripture does shed light on its meaning. In scripture, salvation has been associated with the following:

- Rescue from the dangers of this life (Matt 8:23–27)
- Final entry into heaven (1 Cor 3:15)
- Childbirth (1 Tim 2:15)
- Inclusion in a community or church (Rom 11:14)
- The name of Jesus Christ (Acts 4:12)
- Forgiveness of sins (Luke 1:77)
- Health and healing (Luke 8:48)
- Conversion and acts of charity (Luke 19:1–10)
- Others remind us to work out our own salvation (Phil 2:12)

That the official documents of the Church have not presented a detailed understanding of salvation attests to salvation's mysterious nature. The seven petitions of the Lord's Prayer (Matt 6:9–13) lead to what John Paul II refers to, but does not define as, "integral salvation."[46] It would appear, therefore, that *salvation is the fulfillment of the Lord's Prayer in individuals, communities, and all of God's creation, in this lifetime and in the next.* Salvation is more than membership in a community, more than a single experience,[47] thought, or belief; rather, inspired by God's grace, it is a succession of experiences, actions, and beliefs that reconcile us to one another and to God in this life and in the life to come. The Lord's Prayer presents the sincere will of God, our loving Father, to save us. It is a prayer of salvation that features the need to do God's will, the need for forgiveness, liberation in times of trial and temptation, deliverance from evil, and the need to be nourished daily by a God who is revealed as a loving parent. That this prayer was presented to us by Jesus Christ suggests his knowledge of human need; the Lord's Prayer "is truly the summary of the whole gospel."[48] His prayer summarizes the need of all people who desire to be reconciled with God. It also suggests that he knows how to satisfy our deepest needs.

Any understanding of salvation needs to consider the whole person, whole communities, and all of God's creation in the present and in the world to come. To say that salvation deals with only one or two of these dimensions would limit its meaning. A more complete understanding of salvation would benefit interreligious dialogue, as the concepts referred to above are not unique to Christianity, nor are they only desired by Christians.

God desires all people to know salvation (1 Tim 2:4), and God offers all people the grace needed to be saved. The way to salvation, then, begins with our response, for some through faith and baptism, and for all, through doing God's will, following the dictates of our conscience, and doing what is good in our traditions. Salvation remains multidimensional. It is worldly and otherworldly, personal and communal, and communicates God's great love for creation. Understanding salvation as the fulfillment of the Lord's Prayer in this world and in the next addresses the temporal, spiritual, and universal needs of individuals and communities. The Lord's Prayer "expects an earthly, this worldly realization of God's will…We have a responsibility to imitate God, to follow his lead in forgiving."[49] Salvation is a gift that is concerned with liberation, deliverance, and healing, especially in this world.

Understood this way, salvation relates to men and women of all races, classes, cultures, and religions.

"Jesus means in Hebrew: 'God saves.' At the annunciation, the angel Gabriel gave him the name Jesus as his proper name, which expresses both his identity and his mission. Since God alone can forgive sins, it is God who, in Jesus his eternal Son made man, 'will save his people from their sins.'"[50] Jesus gives us insight into how God loves God's creation. The challenge to Christians, then, is to consider whether we choose to offer a theology of salvation rooted in fear, or a theology of salvation rooted in hope.

For centuries, the fear of damnation permeated official Church teaching on the universal salvific will of God. The resurrection of Jesus communicates a great message of hope as we learn how death can be conquered; how sin can be forgiven and forgotten; and how we can be made anew. Unfortunately, however, official Church teaching continues to reflect this tension between hope and fear. We have seen how, on the one hand, *Dominus Iesus* asserts that members of other religious traditions are in a "gravely deficient situation"[51]—a message of fear—and, on the other hand, *Dialogue and Proclamation* affirms that "it will be in the sincere practice of what is good in their own traditions and by following the dictates of their conscience that the members of other religions respond positively to God's invitation and receive salvation in Jesus Christ"[52]—a message of hope. Are we communicating salvation as a gift of hope, or are we frightening people into accepting it? Is this the salvation that Jesus Christ intended?

Salvation, as understood and taught by Jesus, has universal and inclusive meaning. It is a gift and a process that leads to life and fulfillment in this life and in the next, for all people and for all time. A deeper understanding of salvation, then, will have something more to offer to interreligious dialogue. It will not be an imposition, but a discussion of what salvation means for us. In this sense it can truly be a "dialogue of salvation." Moreover, this dialogue will encourage humble reflection upon past teaching.

Extra ecclesiam nulla salus is an axiom that continues to attract controversy. A renewed understanding of what it means to be "church" helped move salvation outside the limits of the visible church.[53] The Second Vatican Council taught levels of communion and different ways people are related and/or belong to Christ's church. By offering a fuller understanding of salvation, theologians and the magisterium can bring something new to interreligious dialogue. This fuller understanding may shed some light on how the Spirit works in religious traditions to bring salvation to their members

Official Church teaching has established that the Spirit helps religious traditions communicate salvation to their members. In the previous chapters we have seen how *Christianity and the World Religions* affirmed God's desire to save all people; that salvation extends beyond the visible boundaries of the Church; that the Holy Spirit is present in the religions of the world, calling their members forth to receive salvation; and that God will use these religions as a "means" of helping their followers achieve salvation.[54] Nevertheless, more work needs to be done on how these religions are used; on the one hand, the work of the Spirit is affirmed,[55] and, on the other, the salvific function of the religions themselves is affirmed.[56] If the Church can communicate a fuller understanding of salvation to all people, many people may see that the gift of salvation is not just a Christian thing; it is a gift desired for all people.

It would be very confusing to receive a gift from someone and not know what it is. By communicating to all people that salvation is a gift they can experience in their own traditions they may be more inclined to know what it is. Perhaps in offering a fuller understanding of salvation to the religions of the world, the Church can better present its other doctrines, which are fundamentally connected to the one salvation offered to all people.

This one plan of salvation, however, has many implications. One question cannot be ignored: if there is one salvation, do members of other religions experience the same process after death? Just as the official documents of the Church present salvation as a gift that affects life here and now as well as life beyond the grave, it offers other teachings regarding life after death.

Even the doctrine of purgatory can be rethought in light of our discussion on the universal salvific will of God. This doctrine is relevant, because in the Catholic tradition, it is tied to salvation. Salvation is certain for the souls in purgatory; hence, in official Catholic teaching, purgatory is part of God's one plan of salvation. In brief, purgatory is a place of purification and transition for penitent sinners who love God. While there is sin and judgment, God's mercy and forgiveness continue to be extended to all people after death. It is a time of self-awareness, ongoing conversion, and reflection. On the one hand, the Catholic Church teaches that there is one salvation for all people; on the other hand, it teaches that purgatory is part of this plan of salvation. Salvation involves present-day dimensions as well as dimensions that affect the afterlife. Perhaps in clarifying what the Church means by salvation one could establish that the self-knowledge and examination of conscience of the purgatorial state can also occur in this lifetime. Is not the fulfillment of the Lord's Prayer a type of individual and communal purification?

Purgatory might be understood as *the revisiting of our sinfulness, before or after death, through the eyes of reason, truth, mercy, and love.* It would entail a complete awareness of what prevents our fulfillment and union with God—for example, addiction, abuse, exploitation, greed, self-hatred, or selfishness. It would mean not being limited by our own self-pity and biases. It would involve sincere surrender and trust in a God who desires to be close to us, to forgive us, and to be in communion with us. Moreover, for me the transformation that occurs in a place like purgatory is a transformation that is very much tied to what it means to be saved. Recall that I have defined salvation as the fulfillment of the Lord's Prayer in individuals, communities, and all of God's creation in this life and in the life to come. What is said to occur in purgatory, in both official teaching and in the work of various theologians, is not unrelated to this understanding of salvation. After all, salvation is for whole entire and eternal beings. This process, initiated by God's grace, continues with our response until we are perfectly reconciled to God and one another. Self-awareness, spiritual growth, and integration are not unique to Christianity. In the search for God, is it not human fulfillment that many people desire? However, this doctrine, like the one on salvation, must not be presented in a spirit of fear. Rather, the hope for reconciliation with God, our selves, and others should be the focus of any interreligious discussion on purgatory and salvation.

A fear-based theology of salvation cannot succeed in interreligious dialogue. God wills the salvation of all people, but how does a saved person look, think, act, love? What is of interest here is that Christians may be inspired to consider how members of other religions respond to God's grace and see if their own thoughts and actions witness to such faith. Do we seek God with a sincere heart? Do we seek to do God's will? Do we follow the dictates of our consciences? Do we practice what is good in our own traditions? As Jesus requested, do we follow the commandments, love God and our neighbors as ourselves?[57] Do we desire the fulfillment of the petitions of the Lord's Prayer?

Here, Jesus' words in the Gospel of Luke are relevant. Recall his words before the ascension: "Thus it is written, that the Messiah is to suffer and to rise from the dead on the third day, and that repentance and forgiveness of sins is to be proclaimed in his name to all nations, beginning from Jerusalem" (Luke 24:46–47). For me, the key words here are "beginning from Jerusalem." Throughout the Gospels Jesus challenges those in his own community to repent and to do God's will because not everyone who says "Lord, Lord, will enter the kingdom of heaven" (Matt 7:21). Elsewhere he asserts that he was sent "to the lost sheep of Israel" (Matt 15:24). This suggests the need first for in-house evangelization and the conversion of baptized Christians. While the Book of Acts confirms the spread of the gospel to the Gentiles ("And they praised God, saying, 'Then God has given even to the Gentiles the repentance that leads to life,'" Acts 11:18), Jesus desires his mission to be made known to his community first (Luke 24:47).

The gift of salvation is only relevant when it is lived; preaching the gift of salvation is not enough. How can one communicate the gift of the forgiveness of sins if one does not believe it or experience it oneself? The Church is in need of credible witnesses. It appears that Jesus knew that the members of his own community were in more need of his message. Some of them may have believed they knew all there was to know about following God, but like Jesus, John the Baptist proves otherwise: "Do not begin to say to yourselves, 'We have Abraham as our ancestor,' for I tell you, God is able from these stones to raise up children to Abraham" (Luke 3:7–9). The words "beginning in Jerusalem" should inspire Christians as they seek to do God's will.

While the official documents of the Church and theologians affirm the possibility of salvation for members of other religions, Jesus calls for awareness and conversion within one's own tradition, or else "the kingdom of God will be taken away from you and given to a people that produces the fruits of the kingdom" (Matt 21:43). Following Jesus' warning, Christians are challenged to reconsider their own need for repentance, forgiveness, liberation, deliverance, healing, and reconciliation. Jesus' words must not be limited to the context of yesterday; some Christians, in their ambitious desire to preach the gospel to members of other religions, may lose sight of their own need for conversion: "Even though incorporated into the Church, one who does not persevere in charity is not saved...Or if they fail to respond (to the grace of Christ) in thought, word, and deed, not only shall they not be saved, but they shall be more severely judged."[58] Moreover, they may be preaching an experience, of which they have little knowledge, to a group of people who are living it each day in their own religious traditions. Could it not be, following the official teaching of the Church, that members of other religions may be more "saved" than we are? The Church, or the people of God, cannot be the "universal sacrament of salvation,"[59] or sign of salvation, if the people of God do not respond to God's call to salvation. However, before this is achieved the Church must offer a fuller understanding of what it means to be saved.

A clarification of official Church teaching on the universal salvific will of God will improve dialogue and inspire those working and teaching within the Church to witness to what it means to be saved. The need for our bodies, minds, and spirits to be saved or made well is universal.[60] The official documents of the Church affirm the work of the Holy Spirit in other religious traditions. Acknowledging the "salvific function" of other religions would not diminish the "necessity of the Church for salvation,"[61] as Christians are called to be signs of salvation for the world. Christians, through baptism and faith,[62] and members of other religious traditions, through following the dictates of their conscience, doing God's will, and following what is good in their traditions, have been illuminated by God's grace: "No one after lighting a lamp puts it in a cellar, but on the lampstand so that those who enter may see the light" (Luke 11:33). Thus, the fulfillment of salvation, or the Lord's Prayer, in our own communities will serve to liberate others in their own.

The Future of the Discussion

The universal salvific will of God is part of the full doctrine of God and it needs to be taught with clarity and hope. Any suggestion of limitation narrows God's mercy and implies that God's desire to save all people is not universal. If God's intention to save is universal, we must trust that God is acting in all communities and in all people. The wideness of God's mercy must be recovered and proclaimed.

While theologians have tackled the role religions play in the salvation of their members, exactly how religions are used by God has yet to be clarified in official Church teaching. Cardinal Francis Arinze, president of the Pontifical Council for Interreligious Dialogue, addresses this point:

> The theological question today is not whether people who do not belong to the visible Catholic Church can attain salvation. It is theologically certain that they can on certain given conditions. The question is how do they attain salvation. The plurality of religions, the growing knowledge of these religions which Christians have in our times, the limitations of the spread of the church in space and time, and especially the certainty of the salvific will of God for all humanity move the theologian to keep on reflecting on the working out of this divine will for other believers. [63]

Although several theologians have offered their reflections on this topic, it remains controversial. Jacques Dupuis and Peter Phan are two scholars who have addressed this issue, but their work has attracted inquiry and investigation. In 2007, Phan's book *Being Religious Interreligiously: Asian Perspectives on Interreligious Dialogue* was the object of an inquiry by the Congregation for the Doctrine of the Faith. In this book, Phan assigns a positive role for other religions in the salvation of their adherents. Phan, among other prominent theologians, has studied the salvific value of other religious traditions. The universal salvific will of God is now studied in connection to other religions. While Christians affirm the uniqueness of Jesus Christ and the universal presence of the Holy Spirit, the acknowledgment of God's saving action outside the boundaries of Christianity has opened the doors to new debates and questions. It appears that the debate hinges on the use of two prepositions: *by* and *in*. The Church is faced with the implications of three claims studied and addressed by theologians: "People are saved by Jesus Christ in the Church" (exclusivism); "People are saved by Jesus Christ in their own religious traditions" (inclusivism); "People are saved by their own tradition/mediator in their own traditions" (pluralism). This topic remains both challenging and inspiring. The "dialogue of salvation" continues.

Notes

All Second Vatican Council documents are taken from *Vatican Council II: The Conciliar and Post-Conciliar Documents*, edited by Austin Flannery. Northport, NY: Costello Publishing Co., 1992.

The decrees from the pre–Second Vatican Council councils are from *Decrees of the Ecumenical Councils* (vols. I and II), edited by Norman P. Tanner, SJ. Washington, DC: Georgetown University Press, 1990.

Abbreviations Used in the Notes

AG—*Ad Gentes*, Decree on the Mission Activity of the Church, 1965.

DeV—*Dominum et Vivificantem*, Encyclical of Pope John Paul II, On the Holy Spirit in the Life of the Church and the World, 1986.

DH—*Dignitatis Humanae*, Declaration on Religious Freedom, 1965.

DI—*Dominus Iesus*, Declaration on the Unicity and Salvific Universality of Jesus Christ and the Church, 2001.

DP—*Dialogue and Proclamation*, Reflection and Orientations on Interreligious Dialogue and the Proclamation of the Gospel of

Jesus Christ, Pontifical Council for Inter-Religious Dialogue, 1991.

DV—*Dei Verbum*, Dogmatic Constitution on Divine Revelation, 1965.

EN—*Evangelii Nuntiandi*, Apostolic Exhortation of Pope Paul VI, 1975.

GS—*Gaudium et Spes*, Pastoral Constitution on the Church in the Modern World, 1965.

LG—*Lumen Gentium*, Dogmatic Constitution on the Church, 1964.

NA—*Nostra Aetate*, Declaration on the Relation of the Church to Non-Christian Religions, 1965.

ND—J. Neuner and J. Dupuis, eds., *The Christian Faith in the Doctrinal Documents of the Catholic Church*, 7th rev. ed. (New York: Alba House, 2001).

RH—*Redemptor Hominis*, Encyclical of Pope John Paul II, The Redeemer of Man, 1979.

RM—*Redemptoris Missio*, Encyclical of Pope John Paul II, On the Permanent Validity of the Church's Missionary Mandate, 1990.

ST—*Summa Theologiae* of Thomas Aquinas (London: Blackfriars Edition, 1964–76).

UR—*Unitatis Redintegratio*, Decree on Ecumenism, 1964.

Introduction

1. Congregation for the Doctrine of the Faith, *Instruction on the Ecclesial Vocation of the Theologian* (Vatican City: St. Paul Books and Media, 1990), n. 1.

2. See J. P. Schineller, "Christ and Church: A Spectrum of Views" *Theological Studies* 37 (1976): 545–66. See also Allan Race, *Christians*

and Religious Pluralism: Patterns in the Christian Theology of Religions (London: SCM Press, 1983).

3. See Paul F. Knitter, *Jesus and Other Names* (Maryknoll, NY: Orbis Books, 1996).

4. See Jacques Dupuis, *Who Do You Say I Am?* (Maryknoll, NY: Orbis Books, 1994).

5. Lucien Richard, *What Are They Saying About Christ and World Religions?* (New York: Paulist Press, 1981), 4.

6. See LG 1, 9, 48; GS 42, 45; AG 1, 5.

7. LG 14.

8. LG 16.

9. Paul F. Knitter, *No Other Name? A Critical Survey of Christian Attitudes Toward World Religions* (Maryknoll, NY: Orbis Books, 1985), 142.

10. See Paul F. Knitter, *Jesus and the Other Names: Christian Mission and Global Responsibility* (Maryknoll, NY: Orbis Books, 1996). For more on pluralism, see Diana Eck, *Encountering God: A Spiritual Journey from Bozeman to Banares* (Boston: Beacon Press, 1983). See also John Hick, *The Metaphor of God Incarnate: Christology in a Pluralistic Age* (London: SCM Press, 1993).

11. Richard, *What Are They Saying About Christ and World Religions?* 1.

12. Paul F. Knitter, *One Earth Many Religions: Multifaith Dialogue and Global Responsibility* (Maryknoll, NY: Orbis Books, 1995), 30.

13. Karl Rahner, "Universal Salvific Will of God," in *Sacramentum Mundi: An Encyclopedia of Theology*, ed. Karl Rahner et al., vol. 5 (New York: Herder & Herder, 1968), 406. In other words, the freely given grace of God.

14. DV 7.

15. LG 2.

16. Rahner, "Universal Salvific Will of God," 408.

17. However, there are some texts that allude to restoration: 1 Tim 2:4; 4:10; 2 Pet 3:9; 1 John 2:2; Heb 2:9; Titus 2:11; 2 Cor 5:19; John 12:32; 10:16; Col 1:16, 20; Rom 5:18; Acts 3:19–21. For more on *apocatastasis*, see Hans Urs von Balthasar, *Dare We Hope "That All Men Be Saved?"* (San Francisco: Ignatius Press, 1988). Balthasar suggests that hell exists, but it is not final. See also Julian of Norwich, *Showings* (New

York: Paulist Press, 1978). When dealing with the issue of universal salvation, Julian notes that "all will be well."

    18. William G. Most, *Grace, Predestination, and the Salvific Will of God* (Front Royal, VA: Christendom Press, 1997), 69.

Chapter One: Historical Steps toward Inclusivity

    1. *De fide ad Petrum* 37 (PL 65, 703f).

    2. DS 792.

    3. Fourth Lateran Council, 1215, Canon 1 *On the Catholic Faith*, 230 in Tanner.

    4. ND 804.

    5. Council of Basel-Ferrara-Florence-Rome (1431–45), *Bull of Union with the Armenians*, 1439, 551 in Tanner.

    6. Council of Basel-Ferrara-Florence-Rome (1431–45), *Bull of Union with the Copts*, 1442, 578 in Tanner.

    7. ST II-II, q. 2, a. 8, ad 1.

    8. See ST III, q. 69, a. 4, ad 2.

    9. See ST III, q. 69, a. 4, ad 2.

    10. Council of Trent, Decree on Justification, chapter 14, "On the fallen and their restoration," 677 in Tanner.

    11. ND 1010; see 1009–11.

    12. ND 814.

    13. See ND 849.

    14. See Karl Rahner, "Membership of the Church according to the Teaching of Pius XII's Encyclical 'Mystici Corporis,'" in *Theological Investigations*, vol. 2 (London: Darton, Longman & Todd, 1963), 1–88.

    15. The Holy Office, in 1949, issued a letter to Archbishop Richard Cushing of Boston addressing the challenges put forward by a Jesuit named Leonard Feeney. In this letter the teaching of Pius XII is affirmed. The letter makes the distinction between the explicit desire of those who, in an act of faith, join the Church and those who, through an implicit act along with "supernatural" faith, are related to the Church through their longing and desire to do God's will. See ND 1928, 1944, 854–57.

Chapter Two: Magisterial Teaching

1. DV 14.
2. DV 1.
3. Joseph Ratzinger, "Commentary on the Dogmatic Constitution on Divine Revelation," in *Commentary on the Documents of Vatican II*, vol. III, ed. Herbert Vorgrimler (Montreal: Palm Publishers, 1968), 174.
4. Karl Rahner, "Christianity and the Non-Christian Religions," in *Theological Investigations,* vol. 5, trans. Karl H. Kruger (Baltimore: Helicon Press, 1966), 118.
5. For more on Rahner's understanding of Jesus as "absolute savior," see *Foundations of Christian Faith: An Introduction to the Idea of Christianity,* trans. William V. Dych (New York: Crossroad, 1978), 279–80. See also p. 318.
6. See Rahner, "Christianity and the Non-Christian Religions," 131–32. Also "Anonymous Christians," in *Theological Investigations*, vol. 6 (London: Darton, Longman & Todd, 1969), 390–98.
7. Rahner, *Foundations of Christian Faith*, 176.
8. Ibid.
9. Ibid., 316.
10. Ibid.
11. Rahner, "Christianity and the Non-Christian Religions," 121. Rahner defines a lawful religion as "an institutional religion whose 'use' by man at a certain period can be regarded on the whole as a positive means of gaining the right relationship to God and thus for the attaining of salvation, a means which is therefore positively included in God's plan of salvation" (125).
12. Jean Danielou, however, has been considered as the first Western exponent of the fulfillment theory. See *Holy Pagans in the Old Testament* (London: Longmans, Green and Co., 1957).
13. Jacques Dupuis, *Toward a Christian Theology of Religious Pluralism* (Maryknoll, NY: Orbis Books, 1997), 138.
14. Henri de Lubac, *Catholicisme: Les aspect sociauz du dogme* (Paris: Cerf, 1952), 107–10.
15. LG 1, 9, 48.
16. LG 9.
17. LG 4.
18. LG 3.

19. LG 14.

20. LG 16.

21. Ibid.

22. Ibid.

23. Ibid.

24. Ibid.

25. LG 62.

26. LG 16.

27. LG 17.

28. NA 1.

29. NA 2.

30. NA 3.

31. NA 4.

32. Ibid.

33. AG 1.

34. LG 1.

35. AG 1.

36. AG 2.

37. AG 1.

38. AG 3.

39. AG 4.

40. Ibid.

41. AG 9.

42. AG 11.

43. AG 9.

44. LG 17; NA 2.

45. AG 9.

46. AG 11.

47. DH 1.

48. DH 2.

49. DH 3.

50. AG 1.

51. AG 7, 8, 13.

52. AG 7 makes reference to Mark 16:16, which asserts the necessity of faith and baptism.

53. AG 7. See also LG 14.

54. AG 3.

55. AG 7.

56. GS 92.

57. GS 22.

58. Ibid.

59. GS 10, 45.

60. RH 6.

61. Ibid.

62. Ibid.

63. RH 12.

64. DeV 53.

65. See RM 28.

66. See RM 10 and RM 29.

67. RM 9.

68. RM 10.

69. RM 11.

70. RM 5.

71. See RM 28, 29.

72. John Paul II, "To the Plenary Session of the Secretariat of Non-Christians," *Bulletin*. 66, nos. 22–23 (1987): 225.

73. See DP 2. Paul VI introduced this language of "dialogue of salvation" in the encyclical *Ecclesiam Suam*; see articles 72, 73, 75, 76.

74. DP 2.

75. DP 38.

76. See DP 17.

77. Ibid.

78. DP 29.

79. Ibid. This view is repeated in no. 68, where one reads: "They (members of other religions) may in many cases have already responded implicitly to God's offer of salvation in Jesus Christ, a sign of this being the sincere practice of their own religious traditions, insofar as these contain authentic religious values."

80. LG 16.

81. See DP 29, 67.

82. See DP 33 (cf. LG 1).

83. Ibid.

84. DP 38.

85. *Christianity and the World Religions*, 3.

86. Ibid., 16.

87. Ibid., 25.

88. Ibid., 28.
89. Ibid.
90. Ibid., 29.
91. Ibid.
92. Ibid., 39.
93. Ibid., 48d.
94. Ibid., 50.
95. Ibid., 82.
96. Ibid., 83.
97. Ibid., 84.
98. Ibid., 84, 87.
99. Ibid., 85.
100. Ibid.
101. Joseph Ratzinger, "Letter to Bishops' Conferences," *Origins* 30, no. 14 (September 14, 2000): 220.
102. DI 13.
103. Ibid.
104. DI 14.
105. DI 21.
106. AG 11; NA 2.
107. RM 55.
108. DI 22. Reference is Pius XII, *Mystici Corporis*; see DS 3821.
109. DI 22.
110. LG 16.

Chapter Three: Recent Contributions by Catholic Theologians

1. John Paul II, "To the Plenary Session of the Secretariat of Non-Christians," *Bulletin* 66, nos. 22–23 (1987): 225.
2. See bibliography for more sources.
3. Jacques Dupuis, "Universality of the Word and Particularity of Jesus Christ," *Jesuits in Dialogue* (15th International Congress of Jesuit Ecumenists), Kerala, India, August 15–20, 1999, 18.
4. Ibid.
5. Jacques Dupuis, *Toward a Christian Theology of Religious Pluralism* (Maryknoll, NY: Orbis Books, 1997), 24.

6. Jacques Dupuis, "The Truth Will Make You Free: The Theology of Religious Pluralism Revisited," *Louvain Studies* 24 (1999): 28.

7. Ibid.

8. Ibid.

9. Dupuis, *Toward a Christian Theology of Religious Pluralism*, 306.

10. Ibid., 306–7.

11. Ibid., 316.

12. Ibid.; see also p. 318.

13. Dupuis, "Universality of the Word and Particularity of Jesus Christ," 24.

14. Dupuis, *Toward a Christian Theology of Religious Pluralism*, 319.

15. See the first half of *Toward a Christian Theology of Religious Pluralism*, where he examines contributions made by Justin Martyr, Irenaeus, Clement of Alexandria, Origen, and Augustine. Dupuis shows how these early Christian writers believed the *Logos* brought salvation to those living before the Christ-event.

16. Dupuis, *Toward a Christian Theology of Religious Pluralism*, 320.

17. Jacques Dupuis, *Christianity and the Religions: From Confrontation to Dialogue* (Maryknoll, NY: Orbis Books, 2002), 190.

18. Dupuis, "Universality of the Word and Particularity of Jesus Christ," 28.

19. See Paul F. Knitter, "The Vocation of an Interreligious Theologian: My Retrospective on 40 Years in Dialogue," *Horizons* 31, no. 1 (2004): 135–49.

20. Ibid.

21. Ibid.

22. Ibid.

23. Leonard Swidler and Paul Mojzes, eds., *The Uniqueness of Jesus: A Dialogue with Paul F. Knitter* (Maryknoll, NY: Orbis Books, 1997), 80.

24. Paul F. Knitter, *Introducing Theologies of Religion* (Maryknoll, NY: Orbis Books, 2002), 139.

25. Paul F. Knitter, *Jesus and the Other Names: Christian Mission and Global Responsibility* (Maryknoll, NY: Orbis Books, 1996), 38.

26. Knitter, in *The Uniqueness of Jesus*, 15.

27. Ibid.

28. Ibid., 14.

29. Knitter, "The Vocation of an Interreligious Theologian."

30. Knitter, in *The Uniqueness of Jesus*, 11.

31. Knitter, "The Vocation of an Interreligious Theologian."

32. Knitter, in *The Uniqueness of Jesus*, 13.

33. Ibid.

34. Ibid., 174.

35. Knitter, "The Vocation of an Interreligious Theologian."

36. Gavin D'Costa, "Christ, the Trinity, and Religious Plurality," in *Christian Uniqueness Reconsidered: The Myth of a Pluralistic Theology of Religions*, ed. Gavin D'Costa (Maryknoll, NY: Orbis Books, 1990), 23.

37. Ibid., 19.

38. See Gavin D'Costa, "Revelation and Revelations: The Role and Value of Different Religious Traditions," *Pro Dialogo* 85–86 (1994): 161.

39. Gavin D'Costa, *The Meeting of Religions and the Trinity* (Maryknoll, NY: Orbis Books, 2000), 12.

40. Ibid., 23.

41. Ibid., 128.

Chapter Four: Recent Contributions by Other Christian Theologians

1. John Hick, "A Pluralist View," in *Four Views on Salvation in a Pluralistic World*, ed. Stanley N. Gundry, Dennis L. Okholm, and Timothy R. Phillips (Grand Rapids, MI: Zondervan, 1996), 31.

2. See John Hick, *God and the Universe of Faiths: Essays in the Philosophy of Religion* (London: Macmillan, 1973).

3. Hick, "A Pluralist View," 43.

4. John Hick, *A Christian Theology of Religions* (Louisville, KY: Westminster/John Knox Press, 1995), 18.

5. Hick, "A Pluralist View," 44–45.

6. Ibid., 45.

7. Hick, *A Christian Theology of Religions*, 19.

8. John Hick, "Whatever Path Men Choose Is Mine," in *Christianity and Other Religions*, ed. John Hick and Brian Hebblethwaite (Philadelphia: Fortress Press, 1980), 172.

9. John Hick, *God Has Many Names: Britain's New Religious Pluralism* (London: Macmillan, 1980), 122.

10. See John Hick, *Death and Eternal Life* (New York: Harper and Row, 1976).

11. See ibid., 244.

12. See Hick, *God and the Universe of Faiths*, 35.

13. John Hick, "The Possibility of Religious Pluralism: A Reply to Gavin D'Costa," *Religious Studies* 33, no. 2 (June 1997): 161–66.

14. Stanley N. Gundry, Dennis L. Okholm, and Timothy R. Phillips, eds., *Four Views on Salvation in a Pluralistic World* (Grand Rapids, MI: Zondervan, 1995), 12.

15. Ibid., 11.

16. Ibid., 11-12. Particularism is a form of exclusivism.

17. See Clark Pinnock, *Most Moved Mover: A Theology of God's Openness* (Carlisle, UK: Paternoster; Grand Rapids, MI: Baker, 2001).

18. Ibid., 41.

19. Pinnock, "An Inclusivist View," 97.

20. See Clark Pinnock, *A Wideness in God's Mercy: The Finality of Jesus Christ in a World of Religions* (Grand Rapids, MI: Zondervan, 1992).

21. Pinnock, in *The Uniqueness of Jesus*, 119.

22. Pinnock, "An Inclusivist View," 97.

23. Ibid., 106.

24. Ibid., 115.

25. Ibid., 119.

26. Ibid.

27. S. Mark Heim, *Salvations: Truth and Difference in Religion* (Maryknoll, NY: Orbis Books, 1995), 131.

28. Ibid., 160.

29. S. Mark Heim, ed., *Grounds for Understanding: Ecumenical Resources for Responses to Religious Pluralism* (Grand Rapids, MI: Eerdmans, 1998), 11.

30. S. Mark Heim, *The Depth of the Riches: A Trinitarian Theology of Religious Ends* (Grand Rapids, MI: Eerdmans, 2001), 19.

31. Ibid., 3.

32. Ibid., 263–64.
33. For reviews of *Salvations*, see Leo D. Lefebure, "Many Paths, Many Destinations," *Christian Century* 113 F 28 (1996): 236–37. Also, Paul J. Griffiths, "Beyond Pluralism," *First Things* 59 (January 1996): 50–52.
34. S. Mark Heim, *Saved From Sacrifice: A Theology of the Cross* (Grand Rapids, MI: Eerdmans, 2006), 15.
35. Ibid., 295.
36. Ibid., 17.
37. Ibid., 296.

Chapter Five: Conclusions

1. RM 11.
2. GS 22.
3. AG 4.
4. RM 5.
5. RH 6.
6. RH 12; cf. John 3:8.
7. John Paul II, "Message to the Peoples of Asia," in *John Paul II and Interreligious Dialogue*, ed. Byron L. Sherwin and Harold Kasimow (Maryknoll, NY: Orbis Books, 1999), 47.
8. DeV 53.
9. RM 10.
10. DP 29.
11. *Christianity and the World Religions*, 17.
12. Ibid., 24.
13. Ibid., 48d.
14. DI 12.
15. Ibid.
16. Ibid.
17. RM 28 in DI 12.
18. DI 12.
19. Paul F. Knitter, *Introducing Theologies of Religion* (Maryknoll, NY: Orbis Books, 2002), 88.
20. Gavin D'Costa, "Christ, the Trinity, and Religious Plurality," in *Christian Uniqueness Reconsidered: The Myth of a Pluralistic Theol-*

ogy of Religions, ed. Gavin D'Costa (Maryknoll, NY: Orbis Books, 1990), 23. For more on the Spirit and religions, see Joseph DiNoia, "Christian Universalism: The Nonexclusive Particularity of Salvation in Christ," in *Either/Or: The Gospel of Neopaganism*, ed. Carl E. Praeten and Robert W. Jenson (Grand Rapids, MI: Eerdmans, 1993), 37–48.

21. D'Costa, "Christ, the Trinity, and Religious Plurality," 23.

22. Walter Kasper, "Relating Christ's Universality to Interreligious Dialogue," *Origins* 30, no. 12 (November 2, 2000): 326.

23. Ibid.

24. See Amos Yong, *Beyond the Impasse: Toward a Pneumatological Theology of Religions* (Grand Rapids, MI: Baker Academic, 2003). Also, Veli-Matti Karkkainen, *Pneumatology: The Holy Spirit in Ecumenical, International, and Contextual Perspective* (Grand Rapids, MI: Baker Academic, 2002). See also John Zizioulas, *Being as Communion: Studies in Personhood and Church* (London and New York: DLT, 1985). Harold Wells contributes to this discussion as well. See Harold Wells, "The Holy Spirit and Theology of the Cross: Significance for Dialogue," *Theological Studies* 53, no. 3 (September 1992): 476–92.

25. See Yong, *Beyond the Impasse*, 54.

26. For more on the mission of the Holy Spirit and world religions, see Frederick E. Crowe, "Son of God, Holy Spirit and World Religions," in *Appropriating the Lonergan Idea*, ed. Michael Vertin (Washington, DC: Catholic University of America Press, 1989), 324–43.

27. See Georg Khodr, "Christianity in a Pluralistic World—The Economy of the Holy Spirit," *The Ecumenical Review* 23 (1971): 118–28. See also Yong, *Beyond the Impasse*, 86.

28. See Vladimir Lossky, *The Mystical Theology of the Eastern Church* (London: James Clarke, 1957).

29. Yong, *Beyond the Impasse*, 87.

30. Ibid., 86.

31. Ibid., 87. For more see Yves Congar, *The Word and the Spirit*, trans. David Smith (San Francisco: Harper and Row, 1988), chapter 7.

32. See, for example, the discussion on the unbound activity of the Holy Spirit in the section on Jacques Dupuis.

33. See DI 12.

34. See DP 29: "the mystery of salvation reaches out to them (members of other religious traditions) in a way known to God through the invisible action of the Spirit of Christ." Also *Christianity and the*

World Religions, n. 84: "Given this explicit recognition of the presence of the Spirit of Christ in the religions…"

35. See *Christianity and the World Religions*, n. 50

36. See RM 28–29: "It is the Spirit who 'sows the seeds of the Word' present in various customs and cultures, preparing them for full maturity in Christ. Thus the Spirit, who 'blows where he wills' (Jn. 3:8), who 'was already in the world before Christ was glorified'" (AG 4). See also DeV n. 53: "We need to go further back, to embrace the whole action of the Holy Spirit even before Christ."

37. For more information on Orthodox views on salvation outside the Church, see Patrick Barnes, *The Non-Orthodox: The Orthodox Teaching on Christians Outside the Church* (Salisbury, MA: Regina Orthodox Press, 1999).

38. John Paul II, *Crossing the Threshold of Hope* , 136.

39. 1 Tim 2:4; LG 14–17; AG 3.

40. 1 Tim 2:5-6; Acts 4:12; LG 48; GS 43; AG 7, 21; DP 29. Phil 2:5–8 speaks of the need of the incarnation to accomplish salvation. The *Catechism of the Catholic Church* reads: "The Word became flesh for us in order to save us by reconciling us with God, who 'loved us and sent his Son to be the expiation for our sins': 'the Father has sent his Son as the Savior of the world,' and 'he was revealed to take away sins.'" 457, cf. 1 John 4:10; 4:14; 3:5.

41. Matt 7:21; Luke 3:7–9; Matt 19:16; Matt 22:37–40; Matt 21:43; RM 9; RM 10; LG 16; DP 29.

42. GS 22; AG 2; DI 20.

43. See Denis Edwards, *What Are They Saying About Salvation?* (Mahwah, NJ: Paulist Press, 1986). Jerome Theisen writes that the concept of salvation is "exceedingly complex"; however, he does note that "salvation is called the forgiveness of sins, participation in the divine life, union with the person of Christ, freedom, righteousness, peace, entry into the kingdom, active imitation of Jesus, knowledge of the truth, security of hope, love of God, confident faith, resurrection in Jesus, eternal life and vision of God, enlightenment, transformation of the total person and his cosmos, the kindness of the Father, the assistance of God, the word of God, the healing of the mind, the presence of God himself…the process of salvation certainly includes the many aspects of divine healing." See Jerome Theisen, *The Ultimate Church and the Promise of Salvation* (Collegeville, MN: St. John's University

Press, 1976), xviii–xix. In his study of Schillebeeckx, Edwards summarizes the meaning of salvation in the New Testament. Edward Schillebeeckx explores key concepts that link salvation to freedom; redemption; being freed from slavery; liberation from ransom; reconciliation after a dispute; satisfaction and peace; expiation of sins through a sin offering; the forgiveness of sins; justification and sanctification; salvation in Jesus as legal aid; being redeemed for community; being freed for love; being freed for freedom; renewal of persons and the world; life in fullness; victory over alienating and demonic powers. See Edward Schillebeeckx, *Christ: The Christian Experience in the Modern World* (London: SCM Press, 1980), 477–511.

44. Clark Carlton, *The Life: The Orthodox Doctrine of Salvation. An Orthodox Catechesis* (Salisbury, MA: Regina Orthodox Press, 2000), 10.

45. DP 38.

46. RM 11.

47. In his discussion on Augustine and grace, Jean-Marc Laporte discusses the understanding of justification and sanctification in the time of Paul in the New Testament. He notes how some people, in Paul's day, believed that salvation may have occurred in a single experience: "Paul was at odds with enthusiasts and Gnostics of Corinth, for they were under the illusion that with the experience of justification they had already arrived at the pinnacle of Christian life. He points out that justification is only a beginning, that its reality is distorted unless it points beyond itself and leads to a lengthy process of sanctification, a life of faithful service within a world not yet redeemed, and a loving acceptance of others with all their warts and ambiguities. In order to finally possess in salvation the gift he/she has received in justification, the Christian must let go of it in a life of sanctification which imitates Jesus' own *kenosis*." See Jean-Marc Laporte, *Patience and Power: Grace for the First World* (New York: Paulist Press, 1988), 164.

48. *Catechism of the Catholic Church*, 2761, quoting Tertullian, *De Orat.* 10: PL 1, 1165.

49. Benedict T. Viviano, "The Gospel According to Matthew," in *The New Jerome Biblical Commentary*, ed. Raymond E. Brown, Joseph A. Fitzmeyer, and Roland E. Murphy, Student Edition (London: Geoffrey Chapman, 1993), 645.

50. *Catechism of the Catholic Church*, 430.

51. DI 22.

52. DP 29.

53. See UR 4.

54. *Christianity and the World Religions*, 84.

55. RM 9.

56. *Christianity and the World Religions*, 84. See Lutwig Ott, "The Doctrine of the Last Things or the Consummation," in *Fundamentals of Catholic Dogma* (Rockford, IL: Tan Books, 1974), 473–94. In 1999, John Paul II dedicated three Wednesday Audiences to the Church's teaching on heaven, hell, and purgatory. See *L'Osservatore Romano*, weekly edition in English: "Heaven," July 28, 1999, 7; "Hell," August 4, 1999, 7; "Purgatory," August 11/18, 1999, 7. See also Congregation for the Doctrine of the Faith, "Letter on Certain Questions Concerning Eschatology," *Origins* 9, no. 9 (August 1979): 133. Also, International Theological Commission, "Some Current Questions in Eschatology," *Irish Theological Quarterly* 58, no. 3 (1992): 209–43. J. F. X. Cevetello, "Purgatory," in *New Catholic Encyclopedia*, 2nd ed. (Washington, DC: Gale, 2002), 824. R. J. Bastian, "Purgatory in Theology," in *New Catholic Encyclopedia*, 2nd ed. (Washington, DC: Gale, 2002), 825. Anton VanderWalle, *From Darkness to Dawn* (London: SCM Press, 1984), 213. Also Elmar Klinger, "Purgatory," in *Sacramentum Mundi: An Encyclopedia of Theology*, vol. 5 (Dorval and Montreal: Palm Publishers, 1970), 167.

57. Matt 19:16; Matt 22:37–40; Luke 10:25

58. LG 14.

59. LG 1, 9, 48; GS 42, 45; AG 1, 5.

60. The verb *sozo*, or "being made well" or "saved," occurs often in the phrase "your faith has made you well (saved you)"; for example, Mark 5:34; 10:52; Luke 7:50; 17:19; Luke 18:35–43.

61. LG 14.

62. UR 4.

63. Cardinal Francis Arinze, "Catholic Universities/Interreligious Dialogue," *Origins* 27, no. 35 (February 19, 1998), 595.

Bibliography

Aquinas, Thomas. *Summa Theologiae*. London: Blackfriars, 1964–76.

Congregation for the Doctrine of the Faith. *Dominus Iesus*. Declaration on the Unicity and Salvific Universality of Jesus Christ and the Church, 2000. *Origins* 30, no. 14 (2000): 207–14.

———. "Notification: Father Jacques Dupuis' "Toward a Christian Theology of Religious Pluralism." *Origins* 30, no. 38 (March 8, 2001): 606–8.

D'Costa, Gavin. *Theology and Religious Pluralism: The Challenge of Other Religions*. Oxford: Basil Blackwell, 1986.

———. "*Extra Ecclesiam Nulla Salus* Revisited." In *Religious Pluralism and Unbelief*, edited by I. Hamnett, 130–47. London: Routledge, 1990.

———. "Taking Other Religions Seriously: Some Ironies in the Current Debate on the Theology of the Religions." *Thomist* 54 (1990): 519–29.

———. *The Expository Times*, June 1998, 285.

———. "Revelation and Revelations: The Role and Value of Different Religious Traditions." *Pro Dialogo* 85–86 (1994): 161.

———. "Toward a Theology of Religious Pluralism." *Journal of Theological Studies* 49 (1998): 901–14.

———. "Christ, the Trinity, and Religious Plurality." In *Christian Uniqueness Reconsidered: The Myth of a Pluralistic Theology of Religions*, edited by Gavin D'Costa. Maryknoll, NY: Orbis Books, 1990.

————. *The Meeting of the Religions and the Trinity*. Maryknoll, NY: Orbis Books, 2000.

————. *Disputed Questions in the Theology of Religion*. Blackwell: Oxford, 2008.

Dupuis, Jacques. "The Cosmic Christ in the Early Fathers." *Indian Journal of Theology* 15 (1966): 106–20.

————. "Universality of the Word and Particularity of Jesus Christ." In *Jesuits in Dialogue* (15th International Congress of Jesuit Ecumenists), August 15–20, 1999, Kerala, India, 18–32.

————. *Christianity and the Religions: From Confrontation to Dialogue*. Maryknoll, NY: Orbis Books, 2002.

————. "World Religions in God's Salvific Design in John Paul II's Discourse to the Roman Curia (22 December 1986)." *Seminarium* 27 (1987): 29–41.

————. "The Truth Will Make You Free: The Theology of Religious Pluralism Revisited." *Louvain Studies* 24 (1999): 211–63.

————. *Who Do You Say I Am?* Maryknoll, NY: Orbis Books, 1994.

————. *Jesus Christ at the Encounter of World Religions*. Maryknoll, NY: Orbis Books, 1994.

————. *Toward a Christian Theology of Religious Pluralism*. Maryknoll, NY: Orbis Books, 1997.

————. "A Theological Commentary: *Dialogue and Proclamation*." In *Redemption and Dialogue: Reading Redemptoris Missio and Dialogue and Proclamation*, edited by William R. Burrows. Maryknoll, NY: Orbis Books, 1993.

Heim, S. Mark. *Is Christ the Only Way?* Philadelphia: Judson Press, 1985.

————. "Salvations: A More Pluralistic Hypothesis." *Modern Theology* 10 (1994): 341–60.

————. *Salvations: Truth and Difference in Religion*. Maryknoll, NY: Orbis Books, 1995.

————, ed. *Grounds for Understanding: Ecumenical Resources for Responses to Religious Pluralism*. Grand Rapids, MI: Eerdmans, 1998.

————. *The Depth of the Riches: A Trinitarian Theology of Religious Ends*. Grand Rapids, MI: Eerdmans, 2001.

————. "Salvation as Communion." *Theology Today* 61 (2004): 322–33.

————. *Saved from Sacrifice: A Theology of the Cross.* Grand Rapids, MI: Eerdmans, 2006.

Hick, John. *God and the Universe of Faiths: Essays in the Philosophy of Religion.* London: Macmillan, 1973.

————. *Death and Eternal Life.* New York: Harper and Row, 1976.

————. *God Has Many Names: Britain's New Religious Pluralism.* London: Macmillan, 1980.

————. "Whatever Path Men Choose Is Mine." In *Christianity and Other Religions*, edited by John Hick and Brian Hebblethwaite. Philadelphia: Fortress Press, 1980.

————. *A Christian Theology of Religions.* Louisville, KY: Westminster/John Knox Press, 1995.

————. "A Pluralist View." In *Four Views on Salvation in a Pluralistic World*, edited by Stanley N. Gundry, Dennis L. Okholm, and Timothy R. Phillips. Grand Rapids, MI: Zondervan, 1995.

————. "The Possibility of Religious Pluralism: A Reply to Gavin D'Costa." *Religious Studies* 33, no. 2 (June 1997): 161–66.

————. *The Metaphor of God Incarnate: Christology in a Pluralistic Age.* London: SCM Press, 1993.

————. "The Latest Vatican Statement on Christianity and Other Religions." *New Blackfriars.* December 1998.

Hick, John, and Paul F. Knitter, eds. *The Myth of Christian Uniqueness: Toward a Pluralistic Theology of Religions.* Maryknoll, NY: Orbis Books, 1987.

International Theological Commission. "Christianity and the World Religions." *Origins* 27 (1997): 150–66.

————. "The Hope of Salvation." *Origins* 36, no. 45 (2007): 725–46.

John Paul II. "To the Secretariat for Non-Christians," 1979. In *John Paul II and Interreligious Dialogue*, edited by Byron L. Sherwin and Harold Kasimow, 36–37. Maryknoll, NY: Orbis Books, 1999.

————. "To the Plenary Session of the Secretariat for Non-Christians," 1984. In *John Paul II and Interreligious Dialogue*, edited by Byron L. Sherwin and Harold Kasimow, 37–39. Maryknoll, NY: Orbis Books, 1999.

————. "To Representatives of the Various Religions of the World at the Conclusion of the World Day of Prayer for Peace," 1986. In *John Paul II and Interreligious Dialogue*, edited by Byron L. Sherwin and Harold Kasimow, 42–44. Maryknoll, NY: Orbis Books, 1999.

————. *Redemptoris Missio*. Encyclical Letter, 1990. In *The Encyclicals of John Paul II*, edited by J. Michael Miller. Huntington, IN: Our Sunday Visitor, 1996.

————. "To the Plenary Session of the Pontifical Council for Interreligious Dialogue," 1992. In *John Paul II and Interreligious Dialogue*, edited by Byron L. Sherwin and Harold Kasimow, 40–42. Maryknoll, NY: Orbis Books, 1999.

————. *Dominum et Vivificantem*. Encyclical Letter, 1986. In *The Encyclicals of John Paul II*, edited by J. Michael Miller. Huntington, IN: Our Sunday Visitor, 1996.

————. *Redemptor Hominis*. Encyclical Letter, 1979. In *The Encyclicals of John Paul II*, edited by J. Michael Miller. Huntington, IN: Our Sunday Visitor, 1996.

Knitter, Paul F. *Jesus and the Other Names: Christian Mission and Global Responsibility*. Maryknoll, NY: Orbis Books, 1996.

————. "Roman Catholic Approaches to Other Religions: Development and Tensions." *International Bulletin of Missionary Research* 8 (1984): 50–54.

————. "European Protestant and Catholic Approaches to the World Religions: Complements and Contrasts." *Journal of Ecumenical Studies* 12, no. 1 (Winter 1975): 13–28.

————. *No Other Name? A Critical Survey of Christian Attitudes Toward World Religions*. Maryknoll, NY: Orbis Books, 1985.

————. *One Earth Many Religions: Multifaith Dialogue and Global Responsibility*. Maryknoll, NY: Orbis Books, 1995.

————. "Catholics and Other Religions: Bridging the Gap between Dialogue and Theology." *Louvain Studies* 24 (1999): 319–54.

————. *Introducing Theologies of Religion*. Maryknoll, NY: Orbis Books, 2002.

————. "The Vocation of an Interreligious Theologian: My Retrospective on 40 Years in Dialogue." *Horizons* 31, no. 1 (2004): 135–49.

Lombardi, Josephine. *The Universal Salvific Will of God in Official Documents of the Roman Catholic Church*. Lewiston, NY: Edwin Mellen Press, 2007.

Neuner, J., and J. Dupuis, eds. *The Christian Faith in the Doctrinal Documents of the Church*. New York: Alba House, 1996.

Pinnock, Clark. *A Wideness in God's Mercy: The Finality of Jesus Christ in a World of Religions*. Grand Rapids, MI: Zondervan, 1992.

————. "An Inclusivist View." In *Four Views on Salvation in a Pluralistic World*, edited by Stanley N. Gundry, Dennis L. Okholm, and Timothy R. Philips. Grand Rapids, MI: Zondervan, 1995.

————. "Religious Pluralism: A Turn to the Holy Spirit." McMaster Divinity College.

————. *Most Moved Mover: A Theology of God's Openness*. Carlisle, UK: Paternoster; Grand Rapids, MI: Baker, 2001.

Pius IX. *Quanto Conficiamur Moerore*. Encyclical Letter, 1863.

————. *Singulari Quadam*. Allocution, 1854.

Pius XII. Letter to Archbishop Cushing of Boston re: Feeney. In *The Christian Faith in the Documents of the Church*, edited by J. Neuner and J. Dupuis. New York: Alba House, 1996.

————. *Mystici Corporis*. Encyclical Letter on the Mystical Body of Christ, 1943.

Pontifical Council for Interreligious Dialogue and Congregation for the Evangelisation of People. "Dialogue and Proclamation." 1991.

Secretariat for Non-Christians. "The Attitude of the Church towards the Followers of Other Religions: Reflections and Orientations on Dialogue and Mission." *Bulletin* 56/19/2 (1984): 126–41.

Sullivan, Francis A. *Salvation Outside the Church? Tracing the History of the Catholic Response*. New York: Paulist Press, 1992.

Yong, Amos. *Beyond the Impasse. Toward a Pneumatological Theology of Religions*. Grand Rapids, MI: Baker Academic, 2003.

Index

Other Books in This Series